Ungrievable Lives

Ungrievable Lives

*Racism, Risk and Responsibility in
Neoliberal Societies*

Tanisha Spratt

BLOOMSBURY ACADEMIC
LONDON • NEW YORK • OXFORD • NEW DELHI • SYDNEY

BLOOMSBURY ACADEMIC
Bloomsbury Publishing Plc, 50 Bedford Square, London, WC1B 3DP, UK
Bloomsbury Publishing Inc, 1359 Broadway, New York, NY 10018, USA
Bloomsbury Publishing Ireland, 29 Earlsfort Terrace, Dublin 2, D02 AY28, Ireland

BLOOMSBURY, BLOOMSBURY ACADEMIC and the Diana logo are
trademarks of Bloomsbury Publishing Plc

First published in Great Britain 2026

Cover design by Adriana Brioso
Cover image: *Bucket Shop*, 1999 (oil on canvas) © Tilly Willis / Bridgeman Images

A catalogue record for this book is available from the British Library.

A catalogue record for this book is available from the Library of Congress.

ISBN: HB: 978-1-350-40081-8
          PB: 978-1-350-40080-1
          ePDF: 978-1-350-40083-2
          eBook: 978-1-350-40082-5

Typeset by Integra Software Services Pvt. Ltd.
Printed and bound in Great Britain

For product safety related questions contact productsafety@bloomsbury.com.

To find out more about our authors and books visit www.bloomsbury.com
and sign up for our newsletters.

For Betty, Toni, bell, and Maya

Contents

Acknowledgements

Writing this book would not have been possible without the support, wisdom and generosity of many people, groups and networks. I am grateful to the Early Career Research Network in the Faculty of Liberal Arts and Humanities, University of Greenwich for reading and providing crucial feedback on the book proposal. Particular thanks to Angus McNelly for leading those efforts and for keeping us all fed and caffeinated. I am indebted to the Center for Health and Wellbeing at Princeton University for admitting me as a Visiting Research Fellow in 2023, giving me the time and space needed to develop ideas and begin writing in earnest. I am similarly indebted to Atifa Jiwa at Bloomsbury for her unwavering support and belief in this project from start to finish. Thanks to the Department of Global Health and Social Medicine at King's College London for giving me the dedicated time and resources needed to complete this book. I owe special thanks to Anne Pollock, Sarah Hodges, Sarah Milton, Dörte Bemme, Camara Jones and Chanelle Scott for their unwavering enthusiasm and encouragement throughout the writing process. Many thanks to Rima Saini, Amy Chandler, Gareth Thomas and Oli Williams for their support, advice and cheerleading efforts with this book over the past few years.

Each chapter of this book benefitted from international audiences at institutions including the FXB Center for Health and Human Rights at Harvard University and the Sydney Centre for Healthy Societies, University of Sydney. I am thankful to colleagues there for their engagement and feedback. Many other colleagues committed time to reading individual chapters and offering invaluable comments on drafts. Aaron Reeves, Ali Meghji, Antonia Dawes, Rishita Nandigiri, Mê-Linh Riemann, Humera Iqbal, Oli Williams and Helen West – getting this over the finish line was definitely a joint effort!

Although writing can be a solitary endeavour, I never felt alone while writing this book. I am extremely fortunate to have many friends and family members who sustained me along the way. Heartfelt thanks to Jihane Boudiaf and Evelina (Eve) Sepel for lifting my spirits, making me laugh and calming me down when things felt most in flux – I'm so grateful for you both. Thanks to Claire Nixon, Humaira Chowdhury, Isaac Walker, Pippa Ford, Victoria Adams, Mê-Linh Riemann, Garima Sahai, Humera Iqbal and Sarah Milton for distracting me with cake, hugs, trips abroad, hilarious conversations and dedicated quality time when I've needed them most. Much of this book was written in the Members' Room of the British Library; my thanks to Gordon and the other regulars whose cheerful presence kept me company.

I am grateful to Saidiya Hartman for her scholarship, and for the kindness she showed in inviting me to a symposium on Christina Sharpe's work at Columbia University in 2023. Participation in that event reshaped my thinking on grievability in significant ways. I am grateful to Christina Sharpe for her generosity at that event, and for her scholarship more broadly. The writings of Toni Morrison, bell hooks, Maya Angelou, Zadie Smith, Ralph Ellison, Richard Wright, James Baldwin and many others have profoundly shaped my thinking on the questions at the heart of this book. I thank these authors for their courage, dedication and wisdom.

Finally, I thank my parents, Haywood Spratt and Wendy, for their love, intelligence and unwavering support not only during this project, but throughout my life. Having such wonderful parents is a true blessing, and this book is as much theirs as it is mine.

Preface: A Note to the Reader

By the time you read this book it may already seem outdated. The case studies it highlights, selected because they are well-known reference points and indicative of the broader racial politics they encapsulate, may seem old and/or no longer relatable. They may even seem to be of a different era – one that speaks to a time long passed that has little or no contemporary relevance. The case studies chosen for this book are well-known, but they are by no means unique in terms of the broader politics they evoke. Since knowledge of these stories became publicly available countless other people have been subjected to the same conditions and vulnerabilities that have generated the harms and deaths described. The social and political conditions that bring about these harms and deaths have problematic histories that ground their perpetuation, including the belief in biological differences between racialized groups and ideas of inferiority routinely attached to certain racialized bodies. The articulation of these histories – how they are described, rationalized and contextualized – shifts over time and is itself subject to new formations and justifications based on contemporary politics.

At the time of writing, of the five case studies this book highlights only two people are alive – Roxane Gay and Shamima Begum. The others – Kalief Browder, George Floyd and Alan Kurdi – have all died within the last decade. Despite their passing, they continue to have posthumous significance through the ongoing public conversations their deaths evoke(d). These conversations are routinely linked to the conditions that brought about their death, namely: the horrors of mass incarceration and prolonged solitary confinement, the disproportionate levels of police brutality that Black people are subjected to in systemically racist societies and the inhumane migratory routes people fleeing war zones are often forced to take to reach areas of (relative) safety. The social, political and health crises each story evokes did not originate or end with the people spotlighted. Connections between mental health and 'obesity', racism and higher risk of carceral punishment, criminality and citizenship precarity, police brutality and the perceived expendability of Black life, and precarious border crossings that claim the lives of multiple migrants each year existed before, and continue beyond, the specific case studies outlined. The underlying forces driving these different forms of precarity persist, and the actors invested in their continuation largely remain in influential positions that shape local, national and international politics.

When grappling with the misery of what has been, is, and is likely to be, one is often faced with the uncertainty of how to articulate messages of joy and hope in the present. This articulation requires speaking to and past this misery in ways that both acknowledge it and seek to work through it despite its endurance and presumed inevitability. In the midst of the various forms of violence outlined in this book, affected groups and disaffected spectators have been tasked with living in ways that are both meaningful and fulfilling. Depending on one's constitution, this task can generate feelings of unease at best when one successfully creates and enacts strategies for living in a world where many people are unable to live. It requires the simultaneous acknowledgement of one's privilege in being able to enact those strategies and a broader recognition of the structural conditions that prevent others from doing so. Embedded within this logic is an understanding of the conditions that routinely bestow and withdraw humanity to privileged and underprivileged groups, respectively.

At a recent event in London on the global need for reproductive justice I was struck by one participant's succinct framing of this problem. Sitting on stage at around seven months pregnant, this person described her feelings of discomfort when celebrating her impending motherhood during her most recent prenatal ultrasound scan because of the ongoing war in Gaza. Because countless Palestinian children have died (and continue to die) under Israeli occupation and military bombardment, this participant felt both uneasy and bewildered by the celebration of her forthcoming child when relentless violence claims the lives of so many others. The stark contrast between the joy of her own pregnancy and the devastating loss of life in Gaza left her questioning what it means to nurture new life in a world where so many children are denied life.

At the time of writing, the war in Gaza rages on. The Israeli military offensive in Gaza has so far killed over sixty thousand Palestinian people and Israeli armed forces continue to diminish Palestinian health and deny Palestinian life by implementing various blockades to life-saving humanitarian aid (Lukiv and Adams 2025). The Israeli government, led by Prime Minister Benjamin Netanyahu, justifies these actions as acts of self-defence, attributing them to retaliation against Hamas for the violent acts of kidnap, rape and murder perpetrated against roughly 1,450 Israelis on 7 October 2023 (Yosef and Kourdi 2024). When it comes to blocking the distribution of humanitarian aid, the Israeli Defence Forces (IDF) have repeatedly denied these claims or cited concerns about Hamas intercepting aid and profiting from it (Berman 2025). Following this logic, any humanitarian aid that is distributed to Palestinians is seen to risk strengthening the forces that seek to bring about Israel's destruction. As a perceived mode of self-defence, Palestinian killings can be (and often are) framed by Israeli forces as a 'necessary evil' in pursuit of a 'greater good' – namely, the fortification of Israel as a nation state. This position – rejected by many Israeli citizens but upheld by the current Israeli government – prioritizes Israeli life over Palestinian life by framing Palestinian death as an unfortunate but acceptable cost of war waged in the interest of national security.

This is not a new or unique rationale for war or state-implemented violence against targeted groups. Across the globe, positions such as this have been taken to explain, rationalize and justify the expendability of certain lives and the protection of others. The US war in Iraq and Afghanistan following the 9/11 terrorist attacks and Russia's invasion of Ukraine following concerns about the threat of NATO expansion are just two examples of this in recent decades. What *is* unique about the war in Gaza is the silencing it has produced amongst scholars, journalists and public figures who fear expressing support for either side because of the political inferences that may be deduced. For some, speaking in support of Palestine by condemning Israel for its military bombardment in Gaza is, by default, an anti-Zionist position and, therefore, an anti-Israeli one. Because Israel is a Jewish state this position also risks being interpreted as antisemitic by those who conflate anti-Zionism with antisemitism. At different points, there has been little room for an acknowledgement of *both* the violence perpetrated against Israelis on 7 October *and* the mass murder of Palestinians since the war began shortly afterwards. The inability to hold space for both means that international spectators are tasked with choosing which lives are grievable and which are not.

Returning to my earlier point about this book's temporality, by the time this reaches you countless more Palestinians will have died in the war in Gaza, many more people will have died in the war in Ukraine, and the climate crisis will likely continue to present an existential threat that disproportionately affects Black and Brown communities worldwide. In high-income countries like the UK and the US food poverty may have increased, financial investment in essential public services may have decreased, and the health and well-being of marginalized groups may have plummeted further because of steady divestment from life-saving resources.[1] As such, I find myself writing from a strange position that seems to require both fortitude and optimism. As you will see throughout this book, I find it both challenging and problematic to separate optimism from despair because of the ways in which they have historically coexisted. This means that I am reluctant to dwell on the misery of what has been, is, and will likely be without also acknowledging the hope, joy and determination for a better future that keeps us going. When the latter are utilized by and for the oppressed groups they serve, they can offer strategies for living that protect those groups (sometimes momentarily) from the full weight of their ongoing oppression.

It is my hope that while reading this book you the reader, will recognize the bittersweet quality that comes with reconciling the misery of what is with the possibility of what could be. This balance – sometimes dismissed as an inconsequential distraction – has been a stabilizing force for me while writing the book. I hope it will be a stabilizing force for you while reading it.

References

Berman, L. (2025), 'IDF publishes document it says prove Hamas has been confiscating aid as a matter of policy', *The Times of Israel*, https://www.timesofisrael.com/liveblog_entry/idf-publishes-documents-it-says-prove-hamas-has-been-confiscating-aid-as-a-matter-of-policy (accessed 17 July 2025).

Lukiv, J. and P. Adams. (2025), 'Israel blocks entry of all humanitarian aid in Gaza', *BBC News*, https://www.bbc.co.uk/news/articles/c9q4w99je78o (accessed 17 July, 2025).

Yosef, E. and E. Kourdi. (2024), 'Netanyahu insists Israel will defend itself even if "forced to stand alone"', *CNN*, https://edition.cnn.com/2024/05/05/middleeast/netanyahu-icc-warrants-israel-intl-latam (accessed 17 July 2025).

---

[1] Such as healthcare, social housing, state-funded education systems and community programmes.

Introduction

Conceptualizing Grievable Life

On 8 September 2022, the United Kingdom's longest-reigning monarch, Queen Elizabeth II, died of age-related causes at Balmoral Castle. Following her death, the UK formally observed ten days of national mourning, which provoked conflicting responses from members of the public. For some, this period offered an appropriate and necessary opportunity to reflect on Queen Elizabeth's legacy of public service and her contributions to important causes (perhaps most notably overseeing the dismantling of British colonial rule and presiding over a newly formed British Commonwealth). For others, it signified an unnecessary and cumbersome disruption to ordinary proceedings and imposed an unwarranted obligation to observe an event that they did not personally see as tragic. For the latter, Queen Elizabeth's age, high-quality medical care and the presence of her loved ones on her deathbed meant that her passing was as peaceful as one could hope for and far from tragic. Regardless of one's position, this period provided a unique occasion to communally reflect on what it means to formally and publicly mourn a nationally beloved head of state in a democratic country that prides itself on free speech, free will and individual autonomy.

When heads of state preside over countries that have historically subjugated people of colour in the interest of colonial expansion, global dominance and economic power, questions are often raised about the appropriateness of that mourning. In the days leading up to Queen Elizabeth's death, Nigerian Carnegie Mellon professor Uju Anya posted a tweet that later went viral. In this tweet, Anya expressed her wish for Queen Elizabeth to experience an 'excruciating' death because of her position as 'chief monarch of a thieving raping genocidal empire' (Alem 2022). By naming her as such, Anya frames Queen Elizabeth's death in relation to the countless lives that were lost and destroyed through British colonial rule. Queen Elizabeth's role in overseeing this violence and brutality, Anya infers, should preclude any demonstration of mourning.

The relational ties that Anya draws between Queen Elizabeth and the countless deaths that occurred under and in pursuit of British colonial rule are informed by logics of interdependence and vulnerability. 'To be dependent,' philosopher and critical theorist Judith Butler argues, implies vulnerability: one is vulnerable to the social structure upon which one depends, so if the structure fails, one is exposed to a precarious condition. If that is so, we are not talking about my vulnerability or yours, but rather a feature of the relation that binds us to one another and to the larger structures and institutions upon which we depend for the continuation of life.

(Butler 2021: 46)

By arguing that vulnerability is relational because human lives are interdependent, Butler insists on the need to preserve the life of the other to ensure one's own self-preservation. Because we rely on social structures that are formed by other people it is in our interest to preserve the lives of those others so that we can safeguard our own lives and continued ways of life.

As Anya's comment makes clear, recognizing interdependence (in this case, recognizing the (im)moral ties between Queen Elizabeth's reign and the death of Britain's former colonial subjects) does not require genuine interest in, or respect for, subjugated human lives. Indeed, when those human lives are recognized as disposable because they are seen as one of many of similar value in highly populated countries, they are also often rendered disposable within systems that require 'bodies' rather than people to ensure continued modes of production. To borrow a phrase from Giorgio Agamben, subjects seen as replaceable are reduced to 'bare life,' where their existence is viewed in relation to their ability to produce rather than in relation to their subjectivity as human beings. This need for production is not limited to colonial or capitalist logics and/or systems. When reflecting on his military service in his memoir *Spare*, Prince Harry notes that you 'can't kill people if you think of them as people. You can't really harm people if you think of them as people' (Prince Harry 2023). In doing so, he demonstrates how, for some, one's ability to kill during combat relies on one's ability to view one's target as 'non-human'. It is only by doing so that one *can* kill. Reducing people to 'bare life' and conceptualizing them as 'non-human' allows for a moral acceptance of the act of killing that often precludes feelings of guilt and/or injustice that, under different circumstances, might accompany that act.

Why are some lives considered worthy of public mourning while others are not? And how are the ceremonies that afford that mourning constructed in ways that reify what it means to be grievable? Throughout this book, I argue that this issue centres on recognitions of power. By power, I do not exclusively refer to Foucauldian notions of 'sovereign power' that constitute 'top down' forms of state governance (Foucault, 2004). Rather, I refer to a broader understanding of how power is implemented through social influence, political notability and social likeability. Despite an increase in public conversations about the need for, and relevance of, a monarchy in twenty-first-century Britain in the years leading up to her death, Queen Elizabeth's popularity amongst the British public and throughout the British Commonwealth remained largely consistent since her reign began (Elbaum 2022). Recognition of her leadership and role in overseeing the dismantling of British colonial rule in the early years of her reign caused many to remark on her acts of 'public service' as key reasons why her death was *particularly* sad and why it was worthy of national mourning.

Some who remain critical of the monarchy because of its colonial history observed the period of mourning that followed Queen Elizabeth's death because they saw her legacy as *inherited* rather than acquired through individual interest. Many also appreciated what they saw as Queen Elizabeth's attempt to remedy this legacy by forming a Commonwealth that ostensibly promotes an inclusive understanding of how Britain is constituted. At the time of writing, the Commonwealth consists of fifty-six countries across Africa, Asia, the Americas, Europe and the Pacific, and functions as an association of sovereign states that largely consists of the UK and its formerly colonized nations. Or, to use the words of British writer and broadcaster Afua Hirsch, 'the Commonwealth is a vessel of former colonies with the former imperial master at its helm' (Hirsch 2018). Following this logic, viewing Queen Elizabeth as worthy of respect and public mourning because of her advocacy for the Commonwealth is seen by some as both hypocritical and unwarranted. Regardless of one's position, it is difficult to argue against the notion that Queen Elizabeth was (in life and death) grievable.

What makes a grievable life? How is grievability constituted, and to whom is this status conferred? These questions are widely explored through Judith Butler's work on precarity, vulnerability and (non)violence. In their book *Frames of War: When is Life Grievable?* Butler differentiates between lives that are seen to matter and lives that are not, and in doing so sheds light on contemporary workings of biopolitics in Western neoliberal nation states that have the tools and resources to implement mass violence. Lives that are seen to matter during life are also typically viewed as worthy of mourning after they are lost. Certain lives, Butler argues, matter because of the ways in which they are framed, and are constituted through those framings in ways that render that person deserving of, and subject to, public and private acts of mourning. On the other hand, ungrievable lives, Butler argues, are those lives 'that cannot be lost, and cannot be destroyed, because they already inhabit a lost and destroyed zone; they are, ontologically, and from the start, already lost and destroyed, which means that when they are destroyed in war, nothing is destroyed' (Butler 2016: xix). From this, we might consider the countless refugees who undertake the perilous journey across the Mediterranean Sea to reach Europe each year and die in the process, or the tens of thousands of Palestinian civilians who, at the time of writing, are under daily threat of violence and death in Gaza. Rarely do we learn their names, life histories, successes, struggles or ambitions. Mourning each life lost under these circumstances, even when there is motivation to do so, is a difficult task.

For people who are not powerful public figures and who do not have the ability to make any acts of public service known, their position as figures worthy of public mourning is often precarious. In neoliberal societies such as the United Kingdom and the United States (hereafter the UK and the US), one's capacity to be mourned or posthumously seen in ways that are favourable is often dependent on public perceptions of fault or recognitions of innocence when it comes to how that death occurred. Individual health behaviours that produce adverse health outcomes, engaging in 'risky' practices that lead to premature death, and making decisions that result in life-threatening circumstances are just some of the ways in which these perceptions and recognitions preclude or facilitate understandings of the degree to which a person should be mourned.

Media reports or public discourse that questions what a woman was wearing or whether she was being 'flirtatious' in the moments leading up to her sexual assault position that woman as potentially complicit in her assault. In doing so, they render her partially responsible for it and query her position as an innocent victim by suggesting that the assault occurred, in part, through her own actions. In a different but related way, public debates that centre on the role people living with 'obesity'[1] play in any adverse health outcomes they might later experience often bemoan the use of taxpayers' money in remedying those outcomes through publicly funded healthcare services (Spratt 2022). For proponents of this position, people living with obesity are believed responsible for their ill health because they failed to heed advice about recommended health behaviours (such as 'healthy' eating and regular exercise). This logic assumes that, had they adopted those behaviours, they would not have developed obesity and, therefore, would not have become ill. For many, that person's perceived fault in developing their illness renders them undeserving of both public sympathy and the public resources that are needed to remedy their ill health (Good Morning Britain 2023). These examples make clear the importance of recognizing how perceptions of individual responsibility and agency when it comes to health risks shape public recognition of deservedness in evaluating human life.

For people who are seen as 'productive citizens' through their financial, social, cultural or political contributions – or through their *future potential* to contribute in these ways – questions of grievability and the right to be mourned take on additional meaning. When collectively determined, productive citizenship can confer grievability despite the conditions that brought about death even when those conditions would, under different circumstances, render that person blameworthy for their death. In other words, through one's recognized status as a 'productive citizen' one might procure grievability *despite also* being acknowledged as partially responsible for one's death because of one's individual actions. This procurement becomes further complicated when death is brought about through addiction. In February 2014, Hollywood actor Phillip Seymour Hoffman was found dead in his Manhattan apartment following an accidental overdose of a cocktail of drugs including cocaine, amphetamine and benzodiazepine (BBC News 2014). The response to his death from fellow actors, celebrities, public figures and fans was overwhelmingly sympathetic and decidedly mournful, with many simultaneously celebrating his cinematic contributions while acknowledging his long-term struggle with drug addiction. Despite arguably bringing about his own death, Hoffmann's responsibility for it was absolved through acknowledgement of this struggle, which made room for public mourning and the centring of his achievements in public acts of remembrance.

The question of choice when it comes to addiction is a contentious one and one that is beyond the scope of this book. However, I raise it here to prompt consideration of the role that Hoffmann's fame and influence might have played in garnering sympathy and,

---

[1] I use the term 'obesity' to refer to clinical understandings of the health risks associated with being of a higher weight. I acknowledge that this is an offensive term for some who view it as stigmatizing and use it only when referring to clinical interpretations of weight or public understandings of the health risks associated with being of a higher weight.

by extension, widespread mourning following his death. If Hoffmann had died under the same circumstances but without the achievements that he procured throughout his life would his addiction and the role it played in bringing about his death be viewed in the same way? Would public support for his mourning operate in the same way, and would Hoffmann be perceived as grievable in ways that simultaneously allow for his role in arguably bringing about his own death *and* the outpouring of sympathy it generated? Public discourse that renders ordinary people living with addiction responsible for both their recovery and any adverse health outcomes their addiction generates would suggest not. Indeed, according to a report published by The UK Drug Policy Commission (UKDPC) in 2010, ordinary members of the British public typically perceive drug users as 'dangerous, deceitful, unreliable, unpredictable, hard to talk with and to blame for their predicament' (Lloyd 2010: 8). Why, then, are all lives not rendered equally grievable regardless of the contributions individual people make or the reputations individual people garner and cultivate throughout their life? Or, to put it another way, why are some lives rendered grievable and, thus, worthy of sympathy and mourning after they are lost while others are not, even though the circumstances that brought about their death are the same?

These questions are central to the task of this book, which considers common ideas and assumptions that equate grievability with ideas of deservedness, individual responsibility and autonomy in matters of health and illness. Racism plays a central role in shaping, implementing and enforcing these ideas and assumptions. Throughout this book, I argue that grievability is conferred on individuals and populations deemed 'worthy' of mourning, and that this is largely determined by how that person or population is racialized. Some lives, I argue, are seen to matter more than others because of this differential racialization and the (non)status it confers. Grievability is differentially distributed along racial lines in ways that confer and withhold grievability in accordance with racist attitudes, assumptions and perceptions. As Butler notes, '[f]orms of racism instituted and active at the level of perception tend to produce iconic versions of populations who are eminently grievable, and others whose loss is no loss, and who remain ungrievable' (Butler 2016: 24).

Grievability is routinely reified through media reporting and public broadcasting. When deaths occur and are reported in mainstream news outlets, it is often because there is something particularly notable about that death and/or troubling about its occurrence. Both are routinely reflected in the person (or people) who has died in ways that suggest their loss is particularly noteworthy because of *who they are* or *what they have done*. In July 2019, nineteen-year-old Alana Cutland died after falling from a small airplane while on an internship in Madagascar. The inquest into Cutland's death found that she forced open the airplane door and fell because of a psychotic reaction to an anti-malaria drug she had taken in anticipation of her travels. When reporting on this tragic incident, international media outlets framed Cutland's death in ways that rendered it *particularly* tragic given her status as a 'bright' and 'independent' undergraduate student at the University of Cambridge (BBC News 2019). Often referring to her as 'Cambridge student Alana Cutland,' news outlets including the *BBC*, *The Guardian*, *The Daily Mail* and *Fox News* emphasized the tragic circumstances of her death by leading with Cutland's value as a student at an elite and highly selective institution. Because she was a Cambridge student, these outlets infer, her death should be contextualized in relation to her achievements in life and should be understood as particularly tragic given her academic astuteness.

The assumptions that underlie Cutland's status as a Cambridge student (namely her capacity for hard work, intensive labour and high levels of productivity) give rise to a further and more implicit assumption about her potential for productive citizenship had she survived. As a natural sciences student at Cambridge, Cutland might have gone on to work in industries that benefit others through scientific and/or medical advancements. In this way, Cutland's death could be understood as not only a personal tragedy that undoubtedly continues to negatively impact her family and friends, but also a national loss.

It is important to make clear that my aim in using media reportings that frame Cutland's death as particularly grievable given her Cambridge student status is not to suggest that her death is *not* tragic or worthy of mourning. Indeed, any death is clearly both. Rather, I use this example to prompt consideration of why attention is routinely given to the successes and achievements of the person who has died, and how this lends credence to their grievability. Would Cutland's death not be *just* as tragic had she not been a young Cambridge student? And if we agree that it would be (as I hope we would) why is it seen as necessary or important for us to be given this additional information? What added value does it serve from the perspective of news outlets who are charged with constructing the mediatized framings that govern its reporting? What responses did those outlets anticipate from their audience when presented with this information?

Throughout this book, I argue that the degree to which a person is rendered grievable in neoliberal contexts is largely dependent on the ways in which they align, or fail to align, with core neoliberal values and principles including, but not limited to, self-reliance, self-determination, individual responsibility and 'hard work.' In doing so, I utilize B. J. Brown and Sally Baker's articulation of neoliberalism as a governance strategy that was once 'about economics, and premised on an ethos of "small government" and liberalised opportunities for entrepreneurs and investors' but has more recently come to 'embrace desired modes of conduct in enterprising, self-responsible citizens' (Brown and Baker 2012: 6). These citizens are expected to manage their health by complying with neoliberal ideas of self-reliance and autonomy when it comes to health behaviours, healthcare uptake and maintaining their own well-being. By focusing on the relationship between neoliberal attitudes towards health, health outcomes, mortality rates and questions about who is or should be mourned, I consider how these ideas govern grievability through assignations of blame and/or blamelessness. Central to this consideration is a critical evaluation of how victimhood is noted, constructed and legitimized by those in positions of power who reify grievability through biopolitics.

As Butler makes clear, this evaluation is complicated by logics of innocence and culpability that are assigned in war contexts. When the USA invaded Afghanistan and Iraq in 2003, it was both legally legitimized and nationally justified through its framing as a preventative strike against active terrorist regimes in both countries. Enacted in the wake of 9/11, this invasion was framed as a way of eliminating the risk of similar attacks in future (C-SPAN 2013). By positioning this invasion as a way to fortify and ensure US national security, the Bush administration could garner support from those who understood the US to be under imminent, unprovoked and undue threat. This support disregards the inevitable loss of civilian Afghan and Iraqi lives. From this, one might discern a deliberate prioritization of US lives over Afghan and Iraqi lives in ways that reiterate the primacy of US grievability in the global social order. This act, Butler notes, not only does little to quell the possibility of future attack, but also increases the likelihood of retaliatory action. 'In pursuing a wayward military solution,' Butler writes, 'the United States perpetrates and displays its own violence, offering a breeding ground for new waves of young Muslims to join terrorist organisations' (Butler 2020: 23), which could generate future violence.

While many argue that civilian Afghan and Iraqi lives were not afforded equal value to civilian US lives when forming the decision that would inevitably result in their death, throughout the war it was clear that some Afghan and Iraqi lives *were* considered grievable under certain circumstances. In their scholarship on the currency of grief, Jennifer Fluri and Rachel Lehr note the importance of recognizing the value of Afghan civilian deaths when they are brought about by oppressive regimes because they lend legitimacy to some Western policy decisions. 'While Afghan civilian deaths may fall under the U.S. political rhetoric as expendable, collateral and therefore not grievable,' they argue, 'at the same time, they do retain currency … Afghan-aliveness – portrayed through the gendered lens of Taliban and Al-Qaeda imposed suffering – expects a modicum of grievability within U.S framings' (Fluri and Lehr 2015: 24). Women who have been and are oppressed by military regimes that dictate what they can wear and whether they can be educated are particularly likely to elicit sympathy and generate recognitions of grievability from Western women who take these rights for granted. In this way, recognitions of grievability within 'enemy countries'[2] can be understood as, at least in part, conditioned by norms, values and expectations that are set by countries with geopolitical power.

While Butler does not offer an extensive analysis of the relationship between grievability, individual responsibility and neoliberalism, they directly relate the imperative to assume responsibility for oneself to ideas of interdependence that call into question our responsibility to care for others. 'I am certainly not opposed to individual responsibility,' Butler argues, 'and there are ways in which, to be sure, we all must assume responsibility for ourselves. But a few critical questions emerge for me in light of this formulation: am I responsible only to myself? Are there others for whom I am responsible? And how do I, in general, determine the scope of my responsibility?' (Butler 2016: 35). By questioning the nature of individual responsibility in contexts where individuals are, by default, interdependent, Butler queries the practical implementation of individual responsibility when used in service of the self alone. By calling for a recognition of human interdependence,

---

[2] Here I use the term 'enemy countries' to describe nations that are in a state of hostility or conflict with each other, often characterized by opposing political, military or ideological interests.

Butler demonstrates the futility of demands for self-reliance in contexts where we need others to provide us with material resources to live.

The material resources that Butler alludes to, in turn, rely on capitalist modes of production that routinely subjugate and exploit people who are often located in the Global South. Without the mistreatment of exploited peoples, many of us in the West/Global North would be denied both the material luxuries that we regularly enjoy and the everyday necessities that we rely on. Calls to abolish capitalism with the aim of promoting a global recognition of universal grievability would mean creating new ways of living that exist outside of this entrenched economic system. This creation would, in turn, encourage a re-imagining of what our current world might look like if we did not operate under this system, and offer alternative understandings of how we might function under current neoliberal orders. Rather than shaming others for their failure to adopt 'positive' health behaviours, we might more readily lend compassion to those who are unable to do so because of various financial, social and communal constraints through our understanding of mutual interdependence.

Recognizing oneself in the other is not always a straightforward task, nor is it always enough to drive compassion and encourage empathy. Black conservatives in the USA and the UK often deplore the use of tax-money to support Black people who are dependent on that support. Instead, many call for Black people to take greater responsibility for their circumstances and practice self-reliance when it comes to their finances, employment and education (Ondaatje 2010). Higher levels of individual investment in these areas, many argue, will subsequently increase individual control over one's access to healthcare, good quality housing, nutritious foods and other health-promoting resources. This emphasis on individual responsibility is at direct odds with calls to acknowledge forms of systemic racism as inherently responsible for disproportionately poor health outcomes amongst racially minoritized groups. By promoting success stories of Black people who have 'made it' through self-determination and hard work, many Black conservatives seek to both counter and delegitimize the struggles that many Black people face in achieving the same fate (Ondaatje 2010). By showing that it can be done, these Black conservatives discredit Black people who many argue are simply not trying hard enough. In other words, conservative critics who uphold neoliberal values that place a premium on self-reliance and individual responsibility routinely deny the role that systemic racism plays in producing contemporary inequalities by presenting Black people's 'failure' as an individual issue.

Proponents of this belief commonly cite what they see as a growing issue of 'Black victimhood,' a term used to dismiss the economic, social and political effects of systemic racism on contemporary inequities. By upholding the belief that Black people are 'victims' of systemic racism, many argue, proponents risk disincentivizing Black people from aspiring to 'make it' by making them feel that they cannot. In addition, many claim that this argument risks creating a negative mindset amongst Black people who feel 'stuck' or 'trapped' in systems, structures and institutions that were not designed for them and continue to disadvantage them. In this way, critics frame arguments that favour recognizing the impact of systemic racism as decidedly *anti-Black* because those arguments risk promoting Black infantilization and stunting

Black ambition (Reopen US 2020). This critique not only discounts the ways in which Black ambition is routinely formed *despite* the multiple hurdles that systemic racism presents but also, when adopted by people with the power to implement much-needed changes, risks obstructing anti-racist interventions that would work towards achieving racial equity.

Contestations over what it means to be anti-Black – promoting what is seen as a culture of 'Black victimhood' on the political Right and implementing policies and practices that perpetuate racial inequity by those on the political Left – further complicate the relationship between individual responsibility, grievability and health by obscuring the task of meaningfully addressing racial health inequity. Both sides agree that there is an issue, but neither side can agree on how to resolve the issue because they locate its root in different places. When it comes to elected and non-elected government officials who have the power to implement change, where they stand on this divide can determine the chances of achieving social justice in the present and the rate at which it is achieved.

Conceptualizing grievability and Black and Brown (non)life

From the book's title, readers will know that a primary concern throughout this book is to understand how and why, in neoliberal contexts, grievability is racialized. They will also know that these questions are situated in relation to perceptions of risk, responsibility and deservedness that routinely blame the people who are vulnerable to harm for their circumstances. For people who subscribe to neoliberal ideas of self-reliance and autonomy when it comes to health, unavoidable ill health and premature death are often seen as unfortunate and (in some cases) tragic outcomes of circumstances that are largely beyond individual control. In this way, those who fall into this category are routinely understood as blameless and, therefore, deserving of sympathy when they become ill. However, for people who are perceived to have brought their condition on themselves by making 'poor lifestyle choices', declining health and premature death are often framed as the consequences of bad actions.

For racially minoritized people, this rationale is often framed by existing stereotypes of laziness, incompetence and irresponsibility that have historic roots. These logics routinely exist in conjunction with policies and practices that reduce the capacity for racially minoritized people to live healthy lives and avoid premature death at the same rate as their White peers. In her work on the pernicious effects of policies and practices that perpetuate inequity through biopolitical strategies, Lauren Berlant uses the term 'slow death' to describe 'the physical wearing out of a population and the deterioration of people in that population that is very nearly a defining condition of their experience and historical existence' (Berlant 2007: 754). Echoing scholarship on racial 'weathering' that demonstrates how routine exposure to racism can gradually diminish the health of racially minoritized people, Berlant shows how interpersonal and systemic forms of violence are intimately and inextricably connected to everyday forms of living. By calling attention to the steady decline of people within a population who have historically been both disadvantaged and left to suffer, Berlant emphasizes the need to recognize that some lives are (and have always been) valued above others in societies and cultures that willingly promote the lives of some and disregard the lives of others. This distinction, Berlant argues, is both generated and driven by a consistent undercurrent of inequity that is 'muffled in ordinary consciousness' and then revealed as a mainstream feature of everyday life, 'like ants revealed scurrying under a thoughtlessly lifted rock' (Berlant 2007: 761).

Michel Foucault's work on biopolitics adds further nuance to this distinction by highlighting how states selectively invest in the health of certain populations while neglecting or divesting from others. The state's decision to make live and let die, Foucault argues, is informed by political considerations about which populations should receive necessary investment and which should not. These investments are often key to not only human survival but also human flourishing. The (de)valuation of certain lives, particularly within contexts where there is acute competition for resources, is a global issue that cannot be limited to discussions about the USA and the UK. However, what is unique about both countries is how their respective histories of racism and racial inequality have shaped and, in many ways, determined how human life is socially and politically constructed, organized and valued in accordance with perceptions of worthiness. In both countries, Black and Brown people have historically been politically devalued and viewed as unworthy or less worthy of public investment than White people.

Recent shifts within some areas of anti-racist scholarship towards Afropessimism, a theoretical framework that posits Black life as anterior to human life in the ways it is politically conceived and constructed, make clear the need to recognize contemporary workings of biopolitics that are shaped (and in many ways formed) by anti-Black violence. In his book *Afropessimism*, Frank Wilderson argues that Black people are perceived as *functional* beings that reify whiteness through their anteriority to it. Rather than existing as human, he notes, Black people demonstrate what it means to be human through their non-human status. In making this rationale, Wilderson writes that Black people 'are political currency or objects, not political actors or subjects. Subjects have homes, or at least the capacity for some sort of sanctuary. Objects exist as implements, tools, in the psychic life of Human subjects … We are a species of sentient beings that cannot be injured or murdered, for that matter, because we are dead to the world' (Wilderson 2020: 198-9).

By describing Black people as 'currency or objects', Wilderson points to the productive value of Black people who, he argues, function as instruments that are largely used to promote exterior interests. We might use Wilderson's logic to explain the following example: to avoid being labelled a racist, a White person might point to their Black friend and argue that, if they *were* racist, they would not be friends with that person. In this scenario, the Black friend is used to discredit claims of racism and, as such, functions as a form of currency. This function, in turn, dehumanizes the Black friend by reducing them to their value *as* currency, and in doing so positions them as an 'object' rather than as a 'subject.' They are not themselves human, but instead operate *in service of* the human in ways that make clear the productive value of proximal Blackness.

At first glance, Afropessimism offers a clear and simplistic rationale for understanding contemporary logics of ungrievability when it comes to Black life. For Afropessimists like Wilderson, Black lives are not grievable because they are not lives. That is not to say that Black people are not living – after all, Black people breathe, sleep, eat and perform all the other basic human functions that are essential requirements for living. Rather, it is to say that Black people do not live in a humanistic sense of what that living entails. Because Black people do not exist within political or public life, they are prevented from living in ways that would fully qualify their lives as lives. Another reading of this might be that Black people are prevented from living outside the confines of basic human functionality and are thus reduced to a primitive state of being that has historically been used to justify their subjugation. As 'non-humans', Wilderson argues, Black people exist as 'sentient beings' whose purpose in 'life' is to reify *human* life by showing what it is not. As noted by Giorgio Agamben, Black life is 'bare life' and Black ungrievability is rooted in the fact that, to be grievable, one must first have a life that can be recognized as lost (Agamben 1998).

Throughout this book, I challenge Afropessimist articulations of Black 'non-life' by pointing to contemporary forms of what I refer to as acts demonstrating retrospective grievability. I use the term retrospective grievability to describe the conditions under which posthumous grievability can be recognized and conferred upon people who, in life, would have been ungrievable, according to Butler's logic. While Black life can be understood as ungrievable in contexts where Black lives have never mattered, interracial movements that seek to publicly commemorate Black deaths after they have occurred confer posthumous grievability. In other words, I argue that people who were ungrievable when living can, under certain circumstances, *become* grievable when dead. By highlighting the significance of widely known Black deaths that were brought about by state violence (such as George Floyd's murder in 2020) I argue for a re-articulation of how grievability functions within nation states that withhold grievability from some in life and, in certain cases, affirm their grievability through death. In making this point, I ask a set of questions: what motivates posthumous grievability when it is conferred by states that precipitate death? In what ways does posthumous grievability, when bestowed strategically, instigate broader societal and political change? And to what extent do neoliberal logics of (un)deservedness prompt decisions about who succeeds in gaining posthumous grievability and who does not? These questions, among others, guide my discussions throughout this book, particularly in relation to the case studies featured which highlight various racialized responses to death, illness and potential future health risks.

Notes on method and approach

My interest in the topic of grievability and the racial dynamics that underpin it began at the age of seventeen when I first read Toni Morrison's novel *The Bluest Eye*. Throughout this novel, Morrison explores the relationship between external recognitions of beauty and related perceptions of value, making clear how being perceived by others as beautiful can directly lead to positive social outcomes. The novel's pivotal character, Pecola Breedlove, is a dark-skinned Black child from a poor and emotionally dysfunctional family who is routinely taunted and abused by people around her. Surrounded by images that reinforce White beauty norms, as well as adults that in both subtle and unsubtle ways remind her of her 'ugliness,' Pecola prays for blue eyes with the hope that, in having them, she would both *see* beauty in the world and *be seen* as beautiful by the world. Being seen as beautiful, Pecola believes, would positively impact her life by reducing her exposure to violence and generating kind treatment from others.

Halfway through *The Bluest Eye* Morrison introduces a new character, Maureen Peal, who the narrator describes as a 'high yellow dream child with long brown hair braided into two lynch ropes that hung down her back' (Morrison 1999: 60). Unlike Pecola, Maureen is revered for her beauty by those who surround her. She has a lot of friends, is relatively wealthy, well dressed, well-nourished and, in many ways, embodies the aspirations of the Black community she is embedded in. Although she is also Black, Maureen is light-skinned and has loosely coiled hair and green eyes. While reading this book I was struck not only by the unfairness of the differential treatment Pecola and Maureen receive from adults and peers because of their phenotypic differences, but also by the premium placed on self-presentation in societies that view it as emblematic of 'good character.' Rather than recognizing self-presentation as symbolic of access to material wealth, community members view it as a signifier of human value. Maureen's ability to present herself in ways that are visually appealing is suggestive of her family's wealth and importance, while Pecola's inability to do so is suggestive of her family's poverty and insignificance. Unlike Pecola who is routinely seen as 'one of many,' Maureen is seen as unique and is made to feel that her voice, opinions and presence matter. Unlike Pecola, she is grievable because her life is recognized as one that would matter if it were lost.

I do not directly engage with works of fiction in this book, but in some places I use autobiographical accounts that relate feelings of (not) belonging, (in)visibility, and (not) mattering to examine nuanced perceptions of grievability and how they intersect with widescale recognitions of it. In other words, I consider the relationship between local- and national-level grievability politics to note any differences and overlaps between the two. Using memoirs, television interviews, news reports, social media posts and policy documents, I unpack how these relationships unfold through various biopolitical strategies and modes of state abandonment. In doing so, I rely on storytelling as a critical mode of inquiry that grounds theoretical debates in their relevance and applicability within everyday life.

I purposefully chose not to conduct interviews for this book because of the ready availability of online materials that allow me to critically address its core considerations. Following Anne Pollock's ethical rationale for avoiding interviews on sensitive topics when sufficient public materials are available (Pollock 2021: 14), I decided to forgo interviews in favour of public narratives. Pollock's argument that 'interviews might best be reserved for illuminating perspectives that are not already available as public narratives' (Pollock 2021: 14) is a significant one, as it communicates the importance of recognizing the researcher's role in not only highlighting, but also potentially reproducing, forms of suffering. It is my hope that readers of this book will conceptualize the dialectically interwoven themes that it addresses in relation to their own political, social and cultural observations. Far from being unique, each case study presented in this book delineates shared experiences within and between racialized groups, and it is only by recognizing what those shared experiences are that we can begin to create positive and much-needed changes in pursuit of universal grievability.

I approach this topic as a Black, Mixed, cis-gendered, able-bodied, heterosexual woman who holds dual UK and US citizenship. I was born and raised in the UK, but routinely visited family in the USA from a young age. This dual exposure generated an instinctive awareness of the similarities between these countries in terms of how they perceive grievability and its deep connections to citizenship, national belonging and racialization. Before I had a language for it, I recognized that my accent and light skin generated social capital in Black American communities, and that my Blackness and comparably dark skin held negative value for many of my White British peers. I was the first of my family to attend university and I was afforded many of the luxuries and opportunities that a middle-class upbringing gives to those who are fortunate enough to have one. I have attended and worked in some of the most revered universities in the world and have been fortunate enough to pursue a career in academia (I say fortunate because, given the competitive nature of this industry, not everyone who would like to pursue a career in academia is able to do so). I have often considered how my life might or might not be rendered grievable at different stages, and how that might be mapped onto its various turns, pivots and interruptions. In neoliberal societies, we are taught that we earn our value through hard work, perseverance and self-determination, yet the contexts in which we implement these actions are vastly different. Throughout this book, I approach the topic of grievability from both an academic standpoint and an embodied one. My perspective is informed by both academic evaluations of why and how some lives come to matter while others do not, and my experiences of moving through the world. By incorporating both, my aim is to present a holistic conceptualization of contemporary grievability politics that is inherently and unilaterally shaped by legacies of racism and its contemporary manifestations.

Overview of the book

This book features five empirical case studies that have been central to US and UK debates on individual responsibility and accountability in addressing racially minoritized health disparities and death rates. In doing so, it examines how these debates shape, alter and construct grievability politics. Each case study offers unique and valuable insights into the underpinning logics and assumptions that govern neoliberal articulations of health, illness and death. They further illuminate how these logics and assumptions are intimately connected with ideas of deservedness, responsibility and the need for self-actualization. All offer provocations on the question of what it means to live an 'innocent' life, and why protecting 'innocent' life is often prioritized above protecting the lives of those who are believed to be 'at fault' for their condition or predicament.

In Chapter 1, I expand on perceptions of 'choice' and 'risk' when it comes to health-related decision-making by outlining how conditions that are seen to arise from 'poor lifestyle choices', such as obesity, complicate Butler's articulation of grievability. They do so, I argue, by revealing how state and public investment can coincide with a general consensus of apathy that renders those lives both grievable and ungrievable. By simultaneously straddling the two subject positions, I argue that people living with obesity are routinely rendered failures within neoliberal contexts that equate grievable life with productive life. I further argue that racialized perceptions of greed, hypersexuality and excess weight when it comes to Black women in particular decrease public recognition of their grievability after they encounter health complications that are medically associated with it and/or death. This, I argue, is largely due to the ongoing pertinence of racialized stereotypes that present 'fat' Black women as hypersexual and overindulgent and fortify social beliefs that Black women are responsible for their excess weight and are, therefore, undeserving of public sympathy.

In Chapter 2, I consider how public perceptions of blame, shame and accountability shape grievability politics among prison populations. Over the past twenty years, the dehumanizing and destructive impact of mass incarceration on Black and Brown life in the USA has been increasingly documented through film, television and literature. Global recognition of the disproportionately high incarceration rates of young Black men, and the ways in which it contributes to racial disparities in health, has raised questions about the legitimacy of a system that penalizes poorer people who often remain in jail because they cannot afford to bail themselves out (Shah and Seervai 2020). Once they are inside the system and awaiting trial Black men are often rendered invisible (and therefore ungrievable) to external sources while being exposed to increased risk of health conditions including HIV, asthma and depression (Nowotny, Rogers and Boardman 2017). Legally innocent while awaiting trial, they typically become one of many nameless faces that are dismissed as criminals by those who assume they committed the crimes that led to their arrest and imprisonment and are, therefore, deserving of their fate.

In this chapter, I examine the relationship between crime, responsibility and grievability by discussing the case of Kalief Browder, a young Black man from the Bronx, New York who was arrested in 2010 and sent to Rikers Island jail at the age of sixteen for a crime that he did not commit. Maintaining his innocence, Browder repeatedly refused a plea deal that would permit him to return home if he admitted to the offence. Browder remained in jail for three years while awaiting trial before his case was eventually dismissed and he was released. While the injustice of Kalief's case was widely acknowledged after his story was made known, it did little to subsequently change public opinion about the positive correlation between arrest, detention and criminality when it comes to Black men. This, I argue, is largely because of racist beliefs that render Black people in general, and Black men in particular, more likely to commit criminal offences than other racialized groups.

I extend this conversation in Chapter 3 by examining the international impact of George Floyd's murder by Minneapolis police officer Derek Chauvin in 2020, and the degree to which it shaped public perceptions about the relationship between grievability and anti-Black violence. Often referred to as a 'modern-day lynching,' this incident sparked global outrage and subsequent mobilization amongst those who recognized the injustice of a murder that was shaped by racist beliefs about the inherent criminality and expendability of Black life. Throughout this chapter, I explore how right-wing representations of Floyd's 'culpability' as a perceived criminal who was accosted by police officers for 'legitimate reasons' reveal the limits of grievability within the context of Black life. I further show how the global resurgence of Black Lives Matter protests in response to Floyd's death demonstrates a commitment to recognizing Black lives as grievable in contexts where, historically, they have been seen as ungrievable.

Chapter 4 considers the ethical, political and legal implications of citizenship denial for Black and Brown residents, natural born citizens and visa holders who are denied citizenship or have their citizenship revoked because they are perceived as a threat to national security. Throughout this discussion, I consider the health risks associated with this form of state abandonment and how increased vulnerability to those risks speaks to grievability politics. In doing so, I focus on the case of Shamima Begum, a former 'Jihadi bride' who left the Islamic State of Iraq and Syria (ISIS) after it fell to US coalition forces in 2019. Drawing on media coverage of Begum's case and public responses to interviews Begum gave, I evaluate the perceived relationship between culpability, deservedness and grievability when it comes to health and the right to life for people guilty of terrorist offences.

In Chapter 5, I explore the power and limits of social media in generating recognitions of grievability for refugees and internally displaced groups, focusing on the circulation of images of children as innocent victims of violence and displacement in mobilizing public support. In doing so, I centre the case of Alan Kurdi, a Syrian child whose body was found washed up on a Turkish beach in 2015 after he and his family attempted to flee Syria by boat. Drawing on logics of innocence and (un)deservedness to highlight the role that both play in determining grievability for racially minoritized groups, I consider the role of photography in familial commemoration and national mourning.

I conclude this book by reflecting on what it would mean for all lives to be considered grievable, and how this utopic idea might gain traction in a world governed by inequity. In doing so, I move beyond a recognition of contemporary logics of grievability to imagining grievable futures. By taking seriously these utopic possibilities, I discuss ways of imagining grievable futures through private and public anti-racist action and highlight communal ways of promoting grievability by attending to the question of liveable life. In doing so, I reflect on the tensions between the need for self-actualization and the need for systemic political change, and how this synergy is reflected in neoliberal politics that promote individual action over state intervention.

References

Agamben, G. (1998), *Homo Sacer: Sovereign Power and Bare Life*. Stanford University Press.

BBC News. (2014), 'Philip Seymour Hoffman "Killed by Toxic Mix of Drugs"', https://www.bbc.co.uk/news/world-us-canada-26394100 (accessed 9 September 2024).

BBC News. (2019), 'Cambridge Student Alana Cutland "Jumped" from Madagascar Plane', https://www.bbc.co.uk/news/uk-england-beds-bucks-herts-49205138 (accessed 9 September 2024).

Berlant, L. (2007), 'Slow Death (Sovereignty, Obesity, Lateral Agency)', *Critical Inquiry*, 33 (4): 754–80.

Brown, B. J. and S. Baker. (2012), *Responsible Citizens: Individuals, Health and Policy under Neoliberalism*. Anthem Press.

Butler, J. (2016), *Frames of War: When Is Life Grievable?* Verso.

Butler, J. (2020), *Precarious Life: The Powers of Mourning and Violence*. Verso.

Butler, J. (2021), *The Force of Nonviolence: An Ethico-Political Bind*. Verso.

C-SPAN. (2013), 'President Bush Announces Start of Iraq War', https://www.youtube.com/watch?v=5BwxI_l84dc (accessed 9 September 2024).

Elbaum, R. (2022), 'The Life and Legacy of Britain's Longest-serving Monarch', *NBC News*, https://www.nbcnews.com/news/world/queen-elizabeth-life-legacy-uk-monarch-rcna17047 (accessed 9 September 2024).

Fluri, J. L. and R. Lehr. (2015), 'The Currency of Grief: 9/11 Deaths, Afghan Lives, and Intimate Intervention'. In *Economies of Death: Economic Logics of Killable Lief and Grievable Death*, edited by Patricia J. Lopez and Kathryn A. Gillespie, pp. 14–36. Routledge.

Foucault, M. (2004), *Society Must Be Defended: Lectures at the Collége de France*. Penguin.

Good Morning Britain (2023), 'Should We Make Obese People Pay for NHS Treatment?', https://www.youtube.com/watch?v=hLPJ8u8Mc_U (accessed 9 September 2024).

Hirsch, A. (2018), 'What Is the Commonwealth If Not the British Empire 2.0', *The Guardian*, https://www.theguardian.com/commentisfree/2018/apr/17/commonwealth-british-empire-britain-black-brown-people (accessed 9 September 2024).

Lloyd, C. (2010), 'Sinning and Sinned Against: The Stigmatisation of Problem Drug Users', *UK Drug Policy Commission*, https://www.ukdpc.org.uk/wp-content/uploads/Policy%20report%20-%20Sinning%20and%20sinned%20against_%20the%20stigmatisation%20of%20problem%20drug%20users.pdf (accessed 9 September 2024).

Morrison, Toni. (1999), *The Bluest Eye*. Vintage.

Nowotny, K. M., R. G. Rogers and J. D. Boardman. (2017), 'Racial Disparities in Health Conditions Among Prisoners Compared with the General Population', *SSM-Population Health*, 3: 487–96.

Ondaatje, M. L. (2010), *Black Conservative Intellectuals in Modern America*. University of Pennsylvania Press.

Pollock, A. (2021), *Sickening: Anti-Black Racism and Health Disparities in the United States*. University of Minnesota Press.

Prince Harry (2023), *Spare*. Penguin.

Reopen US. (2020), 'Candace Owens: Affirmative Active Hurts Black Students', *YouTube*, https://www.youtube.com/watch?v=-Rx_8T5CaMg (accessed 9 September 2024).

Shah, A. and S. Seervai. (2020), 'How the Cash Bail System Endangers the Health of Black Americans', *The Commonwealth Fund*, https://www.commonwealthfund.org/blog/2020/how-cash-bail-system-endangers-health-black-americans#:~:text=Of%20these%2C%2090%20percent%20%E2%80%94%20the,in%20our%20criminal%20justice%20system (accessed 9 September 2024).

Spratt, T. (2022), 'Reconceptualising Judith Butler's Theory of "Grievability" in Relation to the UK's "War on Obesity": Personal Responsibility, Biopolitics, and Disposability', *The Sociological Review*, 70 (3): 474–88.

Wilderson, F. B. (2020), *Afropessimism*. Liveright.

1

Embodied Trauma and the Burden of Blame: Rethinking Shame and Racialized 'Obesity' Through Roxane Gay's *Hunger: A Memoir of (My) Body*

In February 2012, Trayvon Martin was fatally shot by neighbourhood watch volunteer George Zimmerman while walking home from a convenience store in Sanford, Florida. Contrary to the advice he was given by a 911 dispatcher, Zimmerman pursued Martin and later claimed self-defence as a motive for the killing. During the murder trial, Martin's close friend, nineteen-year-old Rachel Jeantel, was called as a key witness. Jeantel was on the phone with Martin in the moments leading up to his death and claimed to hear part of the altercation. While on the stand Jeantel's responses were short, unclear and, arguably, impertinent. Responding to questions and provocations with 'grunts' and 'sneers,' Jeantel was accused of failing to accurately articulate the events leading up to the shooting and of negatively impacting the prosecution's chances of success.

As a clinically obese, dark-skinned and – to many – seemingly illiterate Black woman, Jeantel was further criticized for failing to embody and perform the markers of what it means to be a 'credible witness.' Jeantel's credibility, many argued, was diminished because her appearance marked her as threatening and untrustworthy to both White and Black audiences in ways that detracted from and delegitimized the evidence she was giving. As noted by Jelani Cobb, '[c]rass assessments of [Jeantel's] weight, looks and intelligence from some white observers competed with a cocktail of vicarious shame, embarrassment, and disdain from some black ones … her appearance, diction, size, and intelligence were an unspoken but all-encompassing part of the proceedings' (Cobb 2013).

The negative criticism Jeantel received for her weight is emblematic of the open disdain many Black women living in larger bodies routinely endure. Stereotypical depictions of 'fat'[1] Black women as hypersexual, masculine, immoral and/or gluttonous have been propagated through anti-Black public discourse since the beginning of

---

[1] I use the terms 'fat,' 'obesity' and excess weight interchangeably in this chapter and in ways that reflect the views of the people being discussed.

the transatlantic slave era (Strings 2019). Through their denigrating and, often, dehumanizing depictions of fat Black women, these stereotypes have often served to uphold racist systems and inequities that mark fat Black women as deviant and undeserving of care. Conversely, certain caricatures of fat Black women have worked to placate White anxieties about 'unruly' and 'hypersexual' Black bodies by presenting them as asexual.

The Black mammy figure – an antebellum caricature of a fat Black maternal caregiver who was often responsible for White child-rearing on slave plantations – depicts the non-threatening Black woman as one who remains subservient, passive and dependent on White patronage. As noted by Andrea Shaw, '[i]n the role as a domestic caretaker, [mammy] represents the ultimate state of black allegiance to whiteness: the ready availability of nurture despite her own economic oppression effected by those she must serve' (Shaw 2005: 146). Following the global resurgence of the Black Lives Matter movement in 2020, visual depictions of the mammy figure were speedily removed from many well-known consumer products that directly profited from them, yet this caricature's circulation remains in much of Black popular culture. Martin Lawrence's performance of Hattie Mae Pierce (also known as 'Big Momma') and Viola Davis's performance of Aibileen Clark are two recent examples of the mammy figure's ongoing cinematic pertinence.

Cinematic depictions of fat Black women often cast them as symbols of greed, poverty and abjection, reinforcing racist beliefs in Black inferiority. The 2009 movie *Precious*, directed by Lee Daniels and endorsed by prominent Black figures including Oprah Winfrey and Tyler Perry, received widespread backlash from anti-racist critics who argued that its overarching depiction of the protagonist – Clareece Precious Jones – relies on racist stereotypes to steer its narrative. Clareece, a clinically overweight, dark-skinned young woman, is repeatedly shown cooking and consuming fatty foods while navigating the familial violence and incestuous rape that have marked her life since early childhood. In one scene, Clareece visits a fast-food restaurant and orders fried chicken while jokingly telling the waitress that she is trying to 'watch [her] figure.' After bringing out a bucket of chicken, the waitress returns to the kitchen and Clareece grabs the bucket and runs out of the restaurant. Halfway down the street Clareece laughs heartily with chicken smeared across her face. She is triumphant because she has successfully stolen the food that will temporarily satiate her hunger.

The symbolic link between fatness, laziness and greed in the public imaginary can (and often does) preclude a recognition of vulnerability in those who gain large amounts of weight in response to trauma and mental ill health. For survivors of sexual violence, weight gain can serve a protective function by allowing that person to build a body that is larger and, thus, more able to withstand physical assault. In this way, weight gain can be understood as an armament that provides some survivors of sexual violence with a preventative strategy. For some of these survivors, gaining weight is also seen as a practice that allows them to become less sexually desirable to potential attackers because it prevents them from adhering to idealized beauty norms that valorize thinness and abhor fatness (Orbach 1998).

Although weight gain can provide psychological protection and resilience for people navigating trauma or mental health challenges, public health guidance on obesity overwhelmingly prioritizes weight loss to promote 'good health.' In doing so, it emphasizes the physical risks associated with being of a higher weight (including coronary heart disease, certain types of cancer and type 2 diabetes) while largely ignoring the potential mental health benefits and embodied strategies of survival that weight gain can offer. For survivors of sexual assault, the mental health benefits of weight gain as a protective strategy may outweigh the associated physical health risks, yet they are still subject to the same public health guidance and interventions as those who have not experienced trauma. The purpose of both is to reduce national obesity rates by encouraging patients to adopt 'positive health behaviours' that encourage regular exercise and healthy eating practices.

Research shows that experiences of sexual violence in childhood can lead to significant weight gain in adulthood. According to one US study conducted by Gustafson and Sarwer in 2004, '[a]mong 511 female, family practice patients in a rural community in the Midwestern United States, those with a history of CSA [childhood sexual abuse] were more likely to be overweight (defined as 40% or more above ideal body weight) and to report having ever been overweight, compared with non-abused controls' (Gustafson and Sarwer 2004: 131). At the age of twelve, writer and cultural commentator Roxane Gay was sexually assaulted by a group of boys in a remote woodland area close to her home in Nebraska. One of Gay's attackers was a former romantic love interest; the rest were unknown to her. After the sexual assault, Gay gained a large amount of weight so that she could become 'solid, stronger, safer' and 'unattractive' to men.

Believing that, by gaining weight, her body would become a 'fortress,' Gay developed disordered eating while she was at boarding school and free from her family's surveillance. When she returned home during school holidays, Gay's family expressed concern and encouraged her to lose weight by engaging in a range of weight-loss practices. After losing weight during her brief stint at home, Gay would return to school and receive compliments from her peers for her weight loss, only to put it all back on by regularly binge-eating. In *Hunger: A Memoir of (My) Body*, Gay notes that, although she felt temporary relief and joy after her initial weight loss, this was quickly met with the impulse to regain the weight she had lost. For Gay, her smaller body was no longer the 'fortress' that would protect her from future harm, which left her feeling unsafe and vulnerable.

In this chapter, I consider how conditions that are seen to arise from 'poor lifestyle choices' (such as consistently eating foods that are low in nutritional content and not exercising) complicate Butler's articulation of grievability by revealing how state and public investment can coincide with a general consensus of apathy that renders those lives both grievable and ungrievable (Spratt 2022). By simultaneously straddling the two subject positions, I argue that people living in larger bodies are often rendered failures within neoliberal contexts that equate grievable life with productive life (Spratt 2022). It is important to note that Roxane Gay's experience differs from that of most people of size. Although she has gone through periods of relative scarcity, Gay has a financial safety net that gives her access to key health-promoting resources when needed. While often misunderstood, she grew up in a loving family that supported and accepted her during her most difficult periods. She also benefitted from opportunities to pursue higher education, build her career and gain public recognition, all of which reflect her privileged position. Yet the presumptions strangers make about Gay's body often obscure these privileges, reducing her to a monolithic understanding of what it means to live in a larger body. For those strangers, it does not matter that her rapid weight gain was not tied to social or economic disadvantage, or that she is highly educated with a strong support network. Gay is typically perceived in the same way as other fat Black women who do not share her privileges.

In this chapter, I argue that racialized perceptions of greed, hypersexuality and 'excess weight' when it comes to Black women further decrease public recognition of their grievability after they encounter health complications and/or premature death. This, I argue, is largely due to the ongoing pertinence of racialized stereotypes that present 'fat' Black women as hypersexual and overindulgent and, in doing so, fortify social beliefs that Black women are responsible for their excess weight and are, therefore, undeserving of public support. By focusing on the experiences of Roxane Gay as told through her memoir *Hunger*, I explore the relationship between fatness, trauma and mental ill health to show how ungrievability is inextricably linked to conditions of disempowerment that disproportionately affect Black women. I further situate this argument in relation to Black feminist scholars whose work centres on the intersections of fatness and race to explore how processes of racialization influence contemporary views about shame, blame, accountability and obesity in Western neoliberal contexts. Additionally, I examine how Black women's efforts to 'fight back' against racist and fat-phobic judgements about their bodies can demonstrate an attempt to present themselves as grievable by asserting value through radical self-acceptance. I conclude this chapter by proposing that public resistance to these efforts signifies a re-articulation of neoliberal understandings of the need to generate self-worth through weight loss and by adopting healthy lifestyle behaviours.

Fat shaming, the 'ideal neoliberal citizen' and the 'obesity epidemic'

In neoliberal economies that view, value and commodify bodies as sites of production, 'fat' bodies are routinely denigrated in ways that mark them as economically unviable (Farrell 2011). Beliefs about 'fat' people being lazy, unmotivated and unintelligent are routinely propagated through media discourse and can shape discriminatory practices in the workplace, making it more difficult for people living in larger bodies to gain employment, promotions or equal pay (Farrell 2011). This discourse can also impact social and familial relationships in ways that encourage shaming behaviours, sometimes with the intention of promoting 'good health' by encouraging that person to better manage their (physical) health by taking responsibility for it (Spratt 2021).

In Western neoliberal contexts, people who are socially recognized as 'fat' are often blamed for their condition and any medical issues that arise from it because they are understood to have directly caused that condition through their 'poor lifestyle choices.' In the case of children who are socially recognized as overweight or obese, parents are often blamed for seemingly failing to regulate their child's food consumption and exercise habits and, therefore, putting their child's health at risk (Greenhalgh 2015). Embedded within this claim is an assumption of control, whereby all people are assumed to be able to *choose* which foods they can eat and the amount of exercise they can undergo on an everyday basis. Proponents of fat shaming commonly refer to freedom of choice to justify their disparaging comments, arguing that consumers have a *choice* about which food items to consume and whether they exercise and are simply *choosing wrong* (Lee and Pausé 2016). This argument is also used to support claims that people living with overweight and obesity are directly responsible for their excess weight and is often utilized to support the argument that fat shaming is beneficial for people living in larger bodies because it could prompt them to change their behaviours (Friedman, Rice and Rinaldi 2020). As noted by US television host Bill Maher in 2019, 'some amount of shame is good. We shamed people out of smoking and into wearing seatbelts. We shamed them out of littering and most of them out of racism. Shame is the first step in reform' (Lee 2019).

Using the biomedical model of obesity to position excess weight as a matter of *health* rather than a matter of *appearance*, proponents of fat shaming often dismiss claims about the adverse effects that this practice can have on the mental health of recipients by citing the relative importance of 'facts over feelings' when it comes to concerns about health (Brown and Baker 2013). By using the word 'fat' to shame people into losing weight, proponents claim that their aim is to improve overall health by calling attention to the various ways in which excess weight presents as a risk factor for certain diseases.

Messages that people who use fat-shaming language and tactics use when communicating the health risks associated with obesity often fail to resonate with the ideological underpinnings of body-positive and fat-activist groups, both of which gained significant online support with the advent of social media in the early-mid 2000s (Afful and Ricciardelli 2015). For many proponents of body positivity, excess weight is largely viewed as an aesthetic concern that is, at best, tangentially linked to health. For many fat activists, body size is an unreliable predictor of health and should not be used in health assessments. Instead, we should aim to dismantle systems that perpetuate fat-phobia and advocate for the acceptance of people who are living in larger bodies. Segments of both groups point to how a clinical focus on the physiological implications of excess weight largely ignores (and risks perpetuating) the mental health effects of weight-related shaming practices (Cooper 2016; Hagen 2019). By prioritizing physical health over mental health, they argue, those who subscribe to the medical model not only overlook the gravity of fat shaming in perpetuating mental illness but also ignore how mental ill health can lead to physical ill health in ways that directly counter their goal of health promotion. For proponents of this view, fat-shaming comments are unanimously interpreted as a form of bullying that purposefully seeks to shame people into holding negative beliefs about their appearance because they do not meet the 'thin' body ideal (Cooper 2016).

The ideal neoliberal citizen is required to both exercise self-restraint and spend excessively to support their local economies. As such, they are often faced with the dilemma of consuming more while seeming to consume less, a phenomenon Deborah Lupton refers to as the 'neoliberal paradox' (Lupton 2018). When it comes to food consumption, one's ability to maintain a slender body type while being encouraged to consume excessive amounts of food is routinely understood as a clear demonstration of one's ability to exercise self-control. Lupton make this point through her argument that, in relation to socio-cultural meanings of the word 'fat,' ideal consumers/citizens 'are able to continue to consume in a context of an abundance of tempting food but also limit their consumption enough to demonstrate their capacity for self-discipline' (Lupton 2018: 34). Through this framework, the ideal neoliberal citizen is perceived as 'thin' and the bad neoliberal citizen is visibly overweight, with their larger bodies seen as an external signifier of their lack of self-control and self-discipline when it comes to food intake and exercise (Fahs 2017: 85).

As well as being expected to regulate their weight to benefit their own health, the ideal neoliberal citizen is often pressured to regulate their weight to minimize any additional 'burden' they might pose to their local and/ or national health care system (Brown and Baker 2013). The financial costs involved in obesity management and treatment for healthcare systems and providers often generate criticism from those who bemoan the use of taxpayers' money to fund the negative outcomes of what they perceive as personal choices that are entirely avoidable. Those who hold this view often demonstrate concern about the fact that this money is being used to support 'self-inflicted' conditions such as obesity and not unavoidable conditions that arise through no fault of the person afflicted, such as certain cancers (Lee and Pausé 2016: 5).[2] Somewhat paradoxically, when considering how obesity is clinically recognized as a risk factor for certain cancers, this attitude can be seen to condone financial investment in treatment for the outcome (cancer) but not for its prevention (obesity).

People living in larger bodies are often viewed as not only self-destructive and gluttonous but also selfish for seemingly prioritizing themselves and their pleasures above others who are dealing with conditions that they did not cause (Greenhalgh 2015). This assumption not only overlooks the many ways in which some people are prevented from maintaining a 'healthy' weight due to various social, financial and environmental factors that are largely beyond individual control, but also fails to account for the ways in which numerous choices, lifestyles and behaviours that are *not* viewed as irresponsible often warrant medical attention without the same moral scrutiny. Sky-divers, skiers, motorcycle drivers and horseback riders are among those who are particularly likely to require medical attention at some point in their lives because of an injury that is cause by something they have chosen to do, yet they are rarely thought of as being a financial drain on the UK's National Health Service (NHS) when they are admitted to hospital or undergo treatment for their injuries. Many fat activists use this point to support their claim that concerns about health in matters

---

[2] Note that certain cancers such as breast cancer routinely prompt this consideration, while others that are seen to arise from poor lifestyle choices and habits (such as lung cancer) do not.

of weight merely mask negative feelings about people living in larger bodies that are rooted in a cultural appreciation of 'thinness' and a dislike of 'fatness' (Cooper 2016).

For many, expressions of 'concern' directed towards people living in larger bodies signify a form of benevolent shaming that ostensibly centres the health of the person being targeted by pointing to the need for health improvement through behavioural change. By making the 'fat' person aware of the risks associated with living in a larger body, the 'concerned' person can feel as though their actions have moral value in ostensibly promoting that person's health. Any negative responses the 'fat' person might then have to these comments can be dismissed as attempts to ignore the science that seemingly supports their claims. This form of 'concern trolling' can take place both online and in person.

In the Hulu television series *Shrill*, the central character, Annie Easton, is routinely denigrated for her body size by people who believe that, through their body shaming, they are communicating their concern for her health. In one episode, a fitness coach approaches Annie in a coffee shop and encourages her to join her fitness classes so that she can lose weight and 'become attractive.' Encouraging her to invest in herself through weight loss, this coach tells Annie that there is a thin person living inside of her who is desperate to come out and *will* come out if she is prepared to put in the effort to lose weight. Responding with a mixture of bewilderment and embarrassment, Annie politely tells her that she will think about it before turning away to get her coffee. Instances such as this are everyday occurrences for people who, because of their size, remain targets of abuse. Throughout *Hunger* Gay conveys similar experiences of concern trolling from both fans and adversaries. In one recollection, Gay discusses how a person removed unhealthy food from her shopping basket while she was grocery shopping as an ostensible act of 'kindness.' This humiliation, Gay argues, demonstrates a pernicious form of fat-phobia whereby fat people are denigrated for making unhealthy choices when it comes to food in ways that operate under the guise of benevolence. By arguing that this chastisement is 'for their own good,' those who infantilize fat people through direct action that causes shame routinely believe that they are demonstrating 'care' through cruelty.

In countries that have state-funded healthcare systems, 'caring' through cruelty can be viewed as not only beneficial for the person who is believed to be risking their own health but also for society at large. Because other people rely on state-funded healthcare systems, proponents argue that reducing the 'burden' individuals pose to health institutions because of their 'poor lifestyle choices' is a matter of national interest because it increases the capacity of those institutions to treat illnesses that are beyond individual control. During the Covid-19 pandemic, UK public health messaging about the link between obesity and increased risk of serious illness and death from Covid-19 prompted widespread fear and panic among many people concerned about the NHS's ability to manage the number of patients being admitted to hospital after contracting the virus. Chronic financial underinvestment and increasing privatization meant that, by the time Covid-19 became an international health emergency, the NHS struggled to cope with the number of patients that required medical care. This, in turn, prompted a fear of resource scarcity, whereby many prospective patients were concerned about whether they would qualify for life-saving treatment if they needed it. These concerns generated a ripe atmosphere for fat-phobia and fat shaming, with many people living in larger bodies being further denigrated for their weight because of the public health crisis (Cooper, Dolezal and Rose 2023).

Because of this threat, the UK government initiated a public health campaign to reduce the number of people living with overweight and obesity in the UK. In doing so, their aim was to reduce the number of hospital admissions for larger patients who, because of their weight, were at increased risk of serious illness and death from Covid-19. Initiated in July 2020, the 'Tackling Obesity Campaign' advocated for weight-loss strategies that rely on dietary changes (referred to as 'simple swaps') to replace unhealthy meals and snacks with healthy ones. In one of the posters that was used to promote this campaign, a large-bodied, dark-skinned Black woman is shown smiling with one hand on her hip and another holding up a plate filled with vegetables and lean meat. The caption beside her lets the viewer know that she is 'cutting down [her] risk' by engaging in healthy eating practices, and the message next to her tells us why. It reads, '[e]xtra weight puts extra pressure on your body. Which makes it harder to fight diseases like cancer, heart disease and now, Covid-19. Losing weight can help reduce your risk. Get help and support to lose weight at nhs.co.uk/betterhealth.' These additional forms of support include access to various online resources, such as a free NHS weight loss plan, healthy eating advice and a Body Mass Index (BMI) calculator that tells users how overweight they are in accordance with clinical guidelines.

Echoing earlier UK public health campaigns that promote and centre the need for individual action when it comes to obesity,[3] this iteration shifts the onus of responsibility for national obesity rates away from the state by affirming it as a private issue. Rather than centring the need for policy reform when it comes to making nutritious food and exercise opportunities more widely available, this campaign advocates for greater individual responsibility when it comes to lifestyle behaviours. The woman pictured is shown at the start of her 'weight-loss journey,' smiling because she has proudly adopted a 'positive' attitude to weight-management by demonstrating her commitment to making recommended changes. She is now in control of her health and has assumed responsibility for it by demonstrating her commitment to making impactful lifestyle alterations. She has become a good neoliberal citizen.

In the USA, public health messaging around obesity has historically adopted similar approaches to the UK by focusing on diet and exercise. Launched in 2010, former First Lady Michelle Obama's *Let's Move!* campaign was quickly criticized for its emphasis on tackling obesity by reducing the individual health behaviours that drive it. Focusing on childhood obesity, this campaign encouraged parents and caregivers to rethink the meals they provide for their children and promote greater activity levels at home. When interviewed about the rationale behind this campaign and why she was keen to make it a priority in her role as First Lady, Obama recollected instances where she and her husband fed their children unhealthy foods because their busy schedules meant that home-cooked meals were difficult to produce. After she began to see the effects this food was having on her children's health, Obama made the decision to

---

[3] For example, the 'change4life' campaign launched in 2009.

invest more time in preparing healthier meals. 'We started making those changes,' Obama claimed, 'short easy changes but they led to some really good results' (The Obama White House 2010). By situating the importance of the campaign in relation to her own experiences, Obama centralizes this issue by presenting it as one that affects families and communities across diverse socio-economic groups. Even for families that can financially afford to follow recommended nutritional advice, time-constraints and work-related commitments can preclude 'good decision-making' when it comes to food.

While the *Let's Move!* campaign echoes UK anti-obesity campaigns through its focus on individual action and autonomy, it differs somewhat in its policy aims and practical approaches. As well as offering parents' information about healthy changes they could make to their diet at home, this campaign focuses on improving food quality in schools and improving access to healthy foods for people living in underserved communities, commonly referred to as 'food deserts.'[4] This focus demonstrates recognition of the need for greater state involvement in making healthy resources accessible by advocating for change at state level. In doing so, it decentres individual responsibility as a key driver of change. Unlike the UK's *Tackling Obesity* campaign, the *Let's Move!* campaign calls for a collaborative effort between the state and its citizens to decrease national obesity rates and improve overall health.

Because of the clinical association between obesity and life-threatening health conditions such as coronary heart disease and cancer, any public health efforts to reduce obesity rates could be understood as altruistic in their endeavour to recognize the grievability of larger people. Through these public health efforts, states that adopt them could be seen to demonstrate a desire to *invest* in people living in larger bodies by increasing their capacity for a longer and 'healthier' life. This is sometimes achieved through financial investment in technologies that, when utilized, can bring about desired changes, such as digital weight-loss applications. Through this investment, the lives of people living in larger bodies are arguably recognized as lives that are worthy of both saving and advancing through state support.

The disparate ways in which that support is offered, and the degree to which the state accepts responsibility for providing that support, demonstrates how biopolitical strategies operate differently in different contexts. While the US approach offers a clear attempt to 'make live' regardless of socio-economic circumstances through targeted state-level interventions, the UK approach demonstrates an attempt to only 'make live' those populations that can financially afford to follow recommended advice. By failing to take responsibility for disproportionately high obesity rates in underprivileged communities through targeted interventions that would make healthy food affordable and exercise opportunities widely available, the UK approach fails to create the conditions that would allow all people to make use of the weight-loss support that it offers. Instead, its approach conveys an investment in 'making live' those who *can*

---

[4] In the USA, 'food desserts' refer to neighbourhoods that do not have local access to supermarkets that sell nutritious foods.

afford to make the recommended changes to their lifestyle behaviours and 'letting die' those who cannot.

This approach further relies on notions of 'good citizenship' alluded to earlier, which are bolstered by ideas of meritocracy and deservedness that sustain persistent inequities in neoliberal economies. Recognizing people who are unable to follow health advice because they cannot afford to do so as blameworthy for their ill health is rooted in the belief that, if they tried harder, they would meet the conditions that would enable good health. Following this logic, if people from socio-economically disadvantaged backgrounds who are living in larger bodies work harder to overcome the structural barriers they face when seeking good health, there is no reason why they would not be able to follow government advice and lose weight through changes to their lifestyle behaviours. By placing the onus of responsibility squarely on the individual, this approach both undermines the pervasive impact these barriers have on the everyday lives of those who are affected by them and overlooks how visible markers of difference have historically shaped access to these resources in ways that have contemporary resonance.

Black women, 'unruly bodies'

In the UK and the USA, Black people are significantly more likely to be clinically recognized as 'overweight' or 'obese' in accordance with BMI than their White peers. According to one UK government report, in 2022, 70.8 per cent of Black adults were classified as overweight or living with obesity, the highest percentage of all racial/ethnic groups (Department for Digital Culture, Media and Sport 2024).[5] Black women who are socially recognized as 'fat' are likely to experience a double burden of weight-related shaming because of both negative views of what it means to be fat and persistent stereotypes about fat Black women that render them unattractive, unintelligent and – in some cases – domineering.

As well as presenting fat Black women as a problem, systems that drive these ideas often centre agency as a primary driver of weight gain and, in doing so, reject claims of deep-rooted prejudice by insisting that size-discrimination is within the remit of individual control. Proponents routinely note that size-discrimination is applicable to anyone who lives in a larger body regardless of gender, age, class or how one is racialized, and therefore cannot be viewed as a phenomenon that unfairly targets one specific group. These beliefs are supported by the core tenets of post-racialism, a theory that argues for a recognition of progress when it comes to racist thinking and attitudes and advances the argument that race is no longer a significant factor in determining a person's opportunities or experiences following the legal gains won by racial justice advocates in the mid-twentieth century (Bonilla-Silva, 2021). As well as overlooking

---

[5] I use the term racial/ethnic groups deliberately here to recognize how these two terms are often conflated in UK health discourse. At the time of writing, the NHS BMI calculator refers to White and mixed groups as 'ethnic' categories when they are, in fact, racial categories.

the myriad ways in which 'old' forms of racist thinking inform contemporary patterns of racial inequity in terms of housing, education, health, etc., beliefs in the universal applicability of size-related discrimination ignore how fat Black women's bodies are often socially viewed in relation to racist tropes and stereotypes mentioned earlier that emerged from racist thinking.

Throughout *Hunger*, Gay provides clear examples of the routine denigration she has faced as a Black woman of size throughout her life, which makes clear the presumption that she is fat because she is lazy, greedy and unable to restrain herself when it comes to food. Knowing that her size is inextricably linked to her experience of sexual violence, readers are consistently aware of the disconnect between presumption and reality as these stories are re-told. By relating this presumption and reality in tandem, Gay challenges the reader to consider their own assumptions about larger people and the underlying cause(s) of their weight gain. This challenge sits in tandem with Gay's acknowledgement that her own actions drove her weight gain, rendering her partially responsible for it. 'At my heaviest,' Gay writes, 'I weighed 577 pounds at six feet, three inches tall. That is a staggering number, one I can hardly believe, but at one point, that was the truth of my body … I don't know how I let things get so out of control, but I do' (Gay 2017: 4). By acknowledging her role in her weight gain, Gay offers an additional challenge to the reader who is then tasked with sitting with any discomfort that arises from simultaneously acknowledging her self-professed culpability while knowing the violent truth of her motivations. This complexity is difficult because it disrupts the binary thinking around significant weight gain that, by default, attributes it to careless lifestyle behaviours driven by greed and uncontrolled impulses. We know that this framework is not only narrow and inadequate, but also harmful as we digest Gay's life history.

For some Black women, racism-induced chronic stress is a leading cause of weight gain because of the positive correlation between chronic stress and increased fat retention. In a study conducted by Yvette Cozier and colleagues in 2014, they found a correlation between perceived everyday racism and obesity incidence, and that this correlation was stronger 'among women with consistent experiences of racism over time' (Cozier et al. 2014: 879–80). When reflecting on the relationship between racism-induced stress and fat retention they write,

> Both animal and human data indicate that chronic exposure to stress can result in neuroendocrine-autonomic dysregulation, which in turn can influence the accumulation of excess body fat … Stress activates the central nervous system and hypothalamic-pituitary-adrenal axis, which, via corticotropin-releasing hormones, stimulates adrenocorticotrophic hormone production and, thus cortisol secretion. Cortisol activates lipoprotein lipase, a regulator of lipid accumulation in adipocytes, increasing fat retention.
>
> (Cozier et al. 2014: 880–1)

If we are to understand that there is a clear correlation between experiences of everyday racism and fat retention, it is important to consider/reconsider the uses of public health messaging that advocates for changes to individual lifestyle behaviours.

Advising racially minoritized people who experience racism-induced stress to eat healthier foods and exercise more regularly does little to address the potential underlying driver of weight gain and, therefore, risks offering an inappropriate strategy for weight loss. When that stress is further compounded by unequal access to health-promoting resources because of their relative financial cost, telling affected groups to 'eat healthier' ignores the barriers that prevent them from doing so.

When it comes to recognizing how Black people's bodies align or fail to align with clinical recognitions of overweight or obesity in accordance with BMI, it is important to note the significance of cultural recognitions of body size and what 'excess weight' signifies in different communities in terms of health, conformity and desirability. Because Black women in the USA and the UK are more likely to hold positive views about their bodies when they are at a larger size than White women (Chithambo and Huey 2013), they are more likely to challenge or reject clinical recognitions of their bodies as 'too big' and at higher risk of adverse health conditions. Living in a larger body is also more likely to be seen as both acceptable and normative in environments where most people are larger in size, and few people conform to normative expectations of 'thinness.'

Colloquial terms such as 'thick' and 'phat' are often used within Black communities to describe women living in larger bodies who are attractive *precisely because* their bodies are larger than idealized 'thin' body norms. The word 'phat' can be colloquially used to describe women who are viewed as 'pretty hot and tempting' (Carter-Francique 2011). The term 'thick' is often used to describe women who are viewed as large but 'well-proportioned,' with fat in areas of the body that are socially acceptable, such as the thighs, buttocks or hips. As noted by body image scholar Elizabeth Hughes, 'thickness describes a "voluptuous [B]lack female body with ample derriere, hips, and thighs," emphasising the distribution of weight in the lower portion of women's bodies' (Hughes 2021: 312). By having a curvaceous body frame, women who embody these terms are often seen to positively emblematize feminine traits that mark their bodies as both desirable and aspirational. Conversely, bodies such as Gay's that supersede the socially fabricated barriers between 'thick'/'phat' and 'fat' are routinely viewed as morally repugnant and unattractive by those who valorize 'thick'/ 'phat' bodies as a beauty ideal.

Terms such as 'thick,' 'phat' and 'fat' are routinely applied to female bodies in ways that demonstrate their subjectivity. Bodies that some might label 'fat' might be recognized as 'thick' by others, and what some might see as 'thick' others might see as 'phat.' Although these distinctions are often unclear, they are important because of the different moral attributes assigned to women – particularly Black women – in relation to them. Whilst 'thick' and 'phat' Black women are often seen as positive examples of organic Black femininity, 'fat' Black women are typically rendered failures within neoliberal economies that seek to discipline 'unruly' Black bodies that fail to conform to normative body types. For many anti-racist fat positive scholars, the latter further demonstrates a recognition of how fat Black bodies continue to be viewed as objects constructed through and by the colonial gaze. As noted by Mary Senyonga and Caleb Luna in their study of music artist Lizzo and her embodied representation of fat female Blackness,

> Intimately tied to the project of colonisation and demonstrative of white fears of corpulence, characterisations of the Black fat female body evince a racial hierarchy that depends on situating Black femininity as a distinct reversal and failure of white femininity ... Where European colonialists boasted of their own slender frames and capacity to 'control' their appetites, and thus also capable of curbing 'base' behaviours, colonial descriptions of the Global South since the sixteenth and seventeenth centuries revealed aversion to and abhorrence of racialised fatness.
>
> (Senyonga and Luna 2021: 272)

According to this logic, social readings of Gay's body as both 'fat' and 'morbidly obese' cannot be separated from her positionality as a Black woman who is morally positioned as the antithesis of hegemonic Whiteness, a construct that valorizes self-control and self-restraint. Recognizing Gay's Blackness and fatness as inextricably linked necessitates a reconsideration of how Gay's (un)grievability is shaped by racist logics and praxis. Through her accounts of routine unsolicited weight loss advice and interventions, Gay offers a recognition of her grievability as one that is conditioned by superficial expressions of concern that are rooted in efforts to make her 'do the right thing' by investing in her health through weight loss. By encouraging her to be a 'good fatty' (a term often used to describe a 'fat' person who is actively trying to lose weight), self-purported advocates and supporters overlook the reason why she initially began to gain weight and the risks to her mental health if she were to lose it.

During periods in her adolescence when Gay lost weight following advice and strict instructions from her parents, returning to school was bittersweet. While she appreciated positive comments about her body size from her classmates, Gay simultaneously experienced a compulsion to regain the weight she lost to recover a feeling of relative safety, often resulting in additional weight gain. Because she lost the feeling of safety and protection that, for her, came with living in a larger body, when her body was smaller Gay once again felt vulnerable and highly visible. Weight gain was, for her, a mechanism that allowed her to feel both detached from her body through its growing unrecognizability and safe in her body through the greater physical protection it offered from men. She writes, 'I became more and more detached from my body, continuing to eat too much and gain weight. I only tried to lose weight when my parents made me or nagged me enough to give dieting a half-hearted try. I didn't care about getting fat. I wanted to be fat, to be big, to be ignored by men, to be safe' (Gay 2017: 75–6).

By noting the intentionality behind her weight gain Gay admits culpability in it and thus challenges the understanding that people who are living in larger bodies are often doing so because of socio-economic disadvantages and other barriers that prohibit the adoption of healthy lifestyles. Moreover, in noting her culpability Gay offers the reader a provocation by positioning herself as both a perpetrator and a victim of her circumstances. If we understand Gay's body size as both a response to the sexual violence she experienced and the result of an active decision that she made to gain weight, to what extent can we view her as responsible for it? When survivors of sexual assault respond to the impact of that experience in ways that others might not choose and/ or might see as 'unhealthy,' should we recognize those responses as 'bad' and blameworthy? Gay further complicates this question by describing her perceived fault in her weight gain as both unequivocal and partial. She writes,

> I did this to myself. This is my fault and my responsibility. This is what I tell myself, though I should not bear responsibility for this body alone … Is my body a crime scene when I already know I am the perpetrator, or at least one of the perpetrators? Or should I see myself as the victim of the crime that took place in my body?
>
> (Gay 2017: 14–18)

By referring to her body as a 'crime scene' Gay presents it as an objective site of 'evidence' that is concurrently marked by violence and efforts towards self-protection. Additionally, Gay claims responsibility for the decisions she made that led to her large body size (most notably excessive food consumption) whilst highlighting her lack of responsibility for the reason behind those decisions (the impact of sexual violence). As both a perpetrator and a victim, Gay troubles the common association between assigning responsibility and recognizing fault in those who practice 'poor' health behaviours by showing how victimhood and agency can co-exist to produce outcomes that are both negative and positive.

Throughout *Hunger* Gay refers to her body as a thing she has been taught to hate because of how it is hated by others, but also as something that provides a fortress that enables a feeling of protection. It is both 'bad' and 'good' in its largeness and all that this represents, and it cannot be reduced to a clinical recognition of how it functions as a risk factor for obesity-related health conditions. With or without her excess weight Gay is at risk of ill health – mental ill health if her shrinking body size leaves her feeling unsafe and physical ill health if any obesity-related health risks materialize into poor physical health outcomes. It is equally important to consider the effects of weight loss on Gay's mental health if she is left feeling vulnerable and exposed as it is to consider the positive effects that weight loss might have on her physical health later in life.

Resistance through existence

In neoliberal economies that seek to discipline 'unruly' bodies through biopolitical modes of governance, merely existing in a larger body can be viewed as an act of resistance. The very fact of one's body as large can be understood as a form of wilful non-compliance, whereby the person in question is presumed to have chosen not to comply with recommended weight-loss advice and/ or purposefully chosen to live an unhealthy lifestyle that has resulted in a larger body. For Black women, this resistance is two-fold as they are often presumed to be both wilfully non-compliant for their fatness and involuntarily non-compliant for their failure to adhere to prescriptive and traditional (White) beauty norms (LeBesco 2004). Both forms of non-compliance mark fat Black women as failures within a neoliberal economy that promotes conformity to normalized aesthetic values (and the material consumption that enables that conformity) as important tenets of 'good citizenship.' Because they exist in bodies that render them subject to both race-based and size-based discrimination, fat Black women often face the daily challenge of having to resist external judgements, criticisms and abuse for existing in the body that they currently live in. Fat Black women who are recognized as actively trying to lose weight through healthy dietary practices and regular exercise sometimes experience a modicum of acceptability among those whose disdain for people living in larger bodies is rooted in a disdain for their perceived 'laziness' and/or lack of self-control. However, many fat Black women routinely struggle to navigate racist and fat-phobic judgements about their bodies that consistently work to denigrate their self-esteem and feelings of self-worth.

When fat women visually present themselves in ways that either outwardly demonstrate a celebration of their bodies or adopt a neutral position by viewing their bodies as neither healthy nor unhealthy they are often met with criticism from those who accuse them of celebrating or 'glorifying' obesity. This 'glorification' centres on the perception that, by being content or happy with their bodies, fat people who refute the idea that their bodies need 'fixing' fail to take the potential health implications of their weight seriously. Additionally, they are often accused of posing a threat to others who might see their body acceptance and/ or celebration as indicative of the idea that it is ok to live in a larger body, which is contrary to medical opinion and advice.

In 2018, White plus-size model Tess Holliday came under scrutiny for a photograph that was featured on the front cover of popular women's fashion and beauty magazine *Cosmopolitan UK*. In this photograph, Holliday is shown wearing a swimsuit while blowing a kiss at the camera. For conservative UK critics such as Piers Morgan, Holliday's presence on this cover, coupled with her unequivocal body confidence, signalled a conscious choice from *Cosmopolitan UK* and Holliday to both celebrate and promote an 'unhealthy' and 'undesirable' body type. Comparing his disdain for this image to the revulsion he would feel if a magazine were to feature an image of an ultra-thin model suffering from anorexia on its front cover, Morgan argued that any celebration of body types that put people at risk of serious illness and/or premature death is both irresponsible and unconscionable (Good Morning Britain, 2018). Yet what Morgan and other critics who echoed similar concerns fail to consider is the limits of this argument when it comes to diverse representation. Would they be as critical if this magazine featured a celebratory image of a woman with terminal cancer on its front cover? Would they oppose a body-positive image of a person in a wheelchair? And what about the countless other models who have appeared on the front cover of magazines with underlying and unseen life-threatening health conditions?

Because of its visibility, fatness is recognized as a pathological problem by those who attribute it to a lack of willpower and motivation, yet its increasing salience as a physical characteristic that can be understood as a marker of bodily autonomy cannot be ignored. Over the past ten years, body positivity, fat acceptance and fat activism have grown in notoriety in online spaces that seek to challenge prevailing medical opinions about the association between excess weight and ill health. For many fat women in these spaces, attempts to subvert normative expectations of female beauty by visually presenting their bodies in ways that challenge how beauty is traditionally conceived represent a form of radical self-acceptance. This is undoubtedly true for Tess Holliday who routinely defends her right to live in her body without seeking to change it (Good Morning America, 2018). However, for women like Holliday, resisting normative expectations of thinness and weight-related criticism through radical self-acceptance is made less challenging than similarly placed women of colour because it does not also involve contending with racist stereotypes.

Singer, songwriter and flutist Lizzo achieved international success in 2019 for her body-positive music, which aims to promote female empowerment through messages of inclusivity, self-care and self-love. As a Black woman living in a larger body, Lizzo demonstrates confidence in her appearance by wearing clothing that showcases her figure and dancing in ways that are often construed as sexually provocative. As a prominent symbol of fat Black female empowerment, Lizzo is often accused of 'glorifying obesity' and promoting an 'unhealthy' body image to her followers and fan base by critics who perceive her as a dangerous and unworthy role model. Not only is Lizzo routinely fat shamed, she is also often the recipient of racist abuse that directly problematizes her fatness in relation to her Blackness. Following the release of her song 'Rumors' with rap artist Cardi B, Lizzo received messages from critics on social media accusing her of conforming to the 'mammy' stereotype because of her body size and upbeat demeanour. By existing in her body, Lizzo was accused of conforming to a trope that has, historically, worked to denigrate Black women by presenting them as functional objects that exist to serve White families and uphold racist structures and systems. Yet this caricature is directly at odds with not only Lizzo's artistry but also the aesthetic that she promotes through this song and its music video.

The premise of this song as a response to 'haters' who spread online rumours about Lizzo and Cardi B about their alleged sexual promiscuity and cosmetic surgical procedures is entirely unrelated to any of the stereotypical tropes associated with the mammy figure. All of the performers in this music video are Black women and there is no mention of acting in ways that place either artist in service to others. In fact, the message promoted through this song is one of both artists reclaiming control over how they are viewed by others and dismissing critics by adopting a nonchalant attitude towards shame-inducing accusations. Not only are all the rumours true, the artists claim, they are also indicative of future behaviours that will continue in the same trajectory despite any criticism.

In her videoed response to the criticism she received, Lizzo points out the discrepancy between her artistry and the mammy stereotype by pointing to the multiple ways in which the two diverge. 'These people who are saying this,' Lizzo argues, 'are probably the same people who are mad when I'm being hypersexual and the mammy trope is actually completely desexualized. So it can't both be true – make it make sense' (Madani, 2021). The fact that this comparison, as Lizzo notes, does not 'make sense' points to the inescapability of this stereotyping for any prominent Black woman who is a public figure and living in a larger body. The very fact that Lizzo not only fails to conform to this stereotype but also, in many ways, directly opposes it through her artistry does not prevent her from being accused of personifying it. Instead, as a Black woman living in a larger body Lizzo is forced to contend with this labelling and the shaming that often accompanies it because of how she visually presents. This labelling and shaming, ironically, often comes from critics who apply racist stereotypes so that they can denounce others for performing them. While all fat women who live in societies that routinely denigrate fatness will likely have to contend with fat shaming at some point in their lives, not all are subjected to the racist abuse that public figures such as Lizzo contend with. White fat women like Tess Holliday, while often reviled, are not situated in relation to racist stereotypes that seek to limit their self-expression and agency in the spaces they exist in by confining them to specific tropes. In this way, their existence through resistance does not require the additional push back that Black women like Lizzo are required to give when met with denigrating messages that seek to diminish their self-worth.

Gay does not subscribe to body positivity in ways that align with subversive forms of rejection. In *Hunger*, she bemoans forms of sizeism that prevent her from living comfortably in her body while noting feelings of weight-related shame. When reflecting on clothing limitations for women of size, Gay describes her reaction as one of 'longing' for the 'shopping trips,' 'sharing clothes with friends' and receiving clothes as a gift that feel unavailable to her (Gay, 2017: 164). This absence is not merely about fashion, it is also about how certain bodies are denied participation in ordinary practices of recognition and care. For Gay, contending with concurrent forms of racism and body shaming from others exists alongside a recognition of the need to feel safer in one's body by becoming bigger. Although Gay is widely criticized for her weight and subjected to similar forms of racist and fat-phobic abuse that other Black women face, her experience of sexual assault and the lasting impact it has had on her relationship with her body means that her resistance through existence involves a different reconciliation. As both a 'vessel' that affords her greater safety in a patriarchal world that routinely threatens violence against women *and* a cause for criticism from fat-phobic and racist detractors, Gay's body can be understood as both necessary for her continued preservation and a 'problem' that, many argue, needs 'fixing.' In its larger form, Gay's body is both a visible emblem of her trauma and a visual indication of her attempts to recover from that trauma, both of which are driven by sexist logics of female submission and domination. Yet it is precisely through her body's visibility that sexist and patriarchal expectations of female submission and dominance are challenged.

Because patriarchal logics can drive wilful non-conformity in female survivors of sexual violence who gain weight in response to their attack, people who uphold patriarchal logics can be understood as the primary impetus behind their own anger and frustration when it is directed towards women living in larger bodies. In other words, by creating the conditions that lead to weight gain in response to trauma and then complaining about women living in larger bodies, proponents of these patriarchal logics can be seen as responsible for their own frustrations. However, rather than recognizing and reckoning with that responsibility, those responsible routinely shift the blame on to women who are responding to their experiences in ways they believe are best suited to their recovery. This shift in responsibility is indicative of contemporary neoliberal responses to systemic issues, whereby the individual is expected to self-manage their response to issues beyond their control in ways that demonstrate personal responsibility and self-control. Not only is this approach an ineffective solution to a systemic problem, it is also potentially harmful if the person who is affected blames themself for not coping in socially sanctioned ways. This onus of responsibility, and its role in self-recovery, further risks reinforcing the systemic inequalities that drive the issue and obscuring the need for broader societal change.

References

Afful, A. A. and R. Ricciardelli. (2015), 'Shaping the Online Fat Acceptance Movement: Talking about Body Image and Beauty Standards', *Journal of Gender Studies*, 24 (4): 453–72.

Bonilla-Silva, B. (2021), *Racism without Racists: Color-Blind Racism and the Persistence of Racial Inequality in the United States*. Rowman & Littlefield.

Brown, B. J. and S. Baker. (2013), *Responsible Citizens: Individuals, Health and Policy under Neoliberalism*. Anthem Press.

Carter-Francique, A. R. (2011), 'Fit and Phat: Black College Women and Their Relationship with Physical Activity, Obesity and Campus Recreation Facilities', *Sport, Education and Society*, 16 (5): 553–70.

Chithambo, T. P. and S. J. Huey. (2013), 'Black/ White Differences in Perceived Weight and Attractiveness among Overweight Women', *Journal of Obesity*, 2013 (1): 1–4.

Cobb, J. (2013), 'Rachel Jeantel on Trial', *The New Yorker*, https://www.newyorker.com/news/news-desk/rachel-jeantel-on-trial (accessed 12 September 2024).

Cooper, C. (2016), *Fat Activism: A Radical Social Movement*. HammerOn Press.

Cooper, F., L. Dolezal and A. Rose. (2023), *COVID-19 and Shame: Political Emotions and Public Health in the UK*. London: Bloomsbury Academic.

Cozier, Y. C., J. Yu, P. F. Coogan, T. N. Bethea, L. Rosenberg and J. R. Palmer. (2014), 'Racism, Segregation, and Risk of Obesity in the Black Women's Health Study', *American Journal of Epidemiology*, 179 (7): 875–83.

Department for Digital Culture, Media and Sport. (2024),'Overweight Adults', https://www.ethnicity-facts-figures.service.gov.uk/health/diet-and-exercise/overweight-adults/latest (accessed 9 September 2024).

Fahs, B. (2017), 'Mapping "Gross" Bodies: The Regulatory Politics of Disgust'. In *Aesthetic Labour: Rethinking Beauty Politics in Neoliberalism*, edited by Ana Sofia Elias, Rosalind Gill and Christina Scharff. Palgrave Macmillan.

Farrell, A. (2011), *Fat Shame: Stigma and the Fat Body in American Culture*. New York University Press.

Friedman, M., C. Rice and J. Rinaldi. (2020), *Thickening Fat: Fat Bodies, Intersectionality, and Social Justice*. Routledge.

Gay, R. (2017), *Hunger: A Memoir of (My) Body*. Corsair.

Good Morning America (2018), 'Tess Holliday Hits Back at "Horrible People" who Body-shame Her', https://www.youtube.com/watch?v=GddirZq2KjY (accessed 21 September 2024).

Good Morning Britain (2018), 'Cosmopolitan Editor Defends Cover Featuring Plus-Size Model Tess Holiday', https://www.youtube.com/watch?v=Xkgtvs_ugDY (accessed 21 September 2024).

Greenhalgh, S. (2015), *Fat-Talk Nation: The Human Costs of America's War on Fat*. Cornell University Press.

Gustafson, T. B and D. B. Sarwer. (2004), 'Childhood Sexual Abuse and Obesity', *Obesity Reviews*, 5 (3): 129–35.

Hagen, S. (2019), *Happy Fat: Taking Up Space in a World that Wants to Shrink You*. 4th Estate.

Hughes, E. (2021), '"I'm Supposed to Be Thick:" Managing Body Image Anxieties among Black American Women', *Journal of Black Studies*, 52 (3): 310–30.

LeBesco, L. (2004), *Revolting Bodies? The Struggle to Redefine Fat Identity*. University of Massachusetts Press.

Lee, B. Y. (2019), 'Bill Maher Asks People to Fat Shame More, Here Is The Response', *Forbes*, https://www.forbes.com/sites/brucelee/2019/09/15/bill-maher-asks-people-to-fat-shame-more-here-is-the-response (accessed 20 September 2024).

Lee, J. A. and C. Pausé. (2016), 'Stigma in Practice: Barriers to Health for Fat Women', *Frontiers in Psychology*, 7, doi: 10.3389/fpsyg.2016.02063.

Lupton, D. (2018), *Fat*. 2nd ed. Routledge.

Madani, D. (2021), 'Lizzo Tearfully Calls Out "Fatphobic" and "Racist" Hate Following "Rumors" Release', *NBC News*, https://www.nbcnews.com/pop-culture/pop-culture-news/lizzo-tearfully-calls-out-fatphobic-racist-hate-following-rumors-release-n1276920 (accessed 20 September 2024).

Orbach, S. (1998), *Fat Is a Feminist Issue*. Arrow Books.

Senyonga, M. and C. Luna. (2021), "'If I'm Shinin', Everybody Gonna Shine:" Centering Black Fat Women and Femmes within Body and Fat Positivity', *Fat Studies*, 10 (3): 268-82.

Shaw, A. (2005), 'The Other Side of the Looking Glass: The Marginalisation of Fatness and Blackness in the Construction of Gender Identity', *Social Semiotics*, 15 (2): 143-52.

Spratt, T. (2021), 'Understanding "Fat Shaming" in a Neoliberal Era: Performativity, Healthism and the UK's "Obesity Epidemic"', *Feminist Theory*, 24 (1): 86-101.

Spratt, T. (2022), 'Reconceptualising Judith Butler's Theory of "Grievability" in Relation to the UK's "War on Obesity": Personal Responsibility, Biopolitics and Disposability', *The Sociological Review*, 70 (3): 474-88.

Strings, S. (2019), *Fearing the Black Body: The Racial Origins of Fat Phobia*. New York University Press.

The Obama White House. (2010), 'The First Lady Introduces Let's Move', https://www.youtube.com/watch?v=2oBeuSCfGeg (accessed 10 September 2024).

2

Ungrievability and Mass Incarceration: The Tragic Death of Kalief Browder

There is a house on Prospect Avenue in the Bronx, New York City, that once had a growing ivy bush creeping along its top left-hand window. This bush, gathered at the edge of the house, hung delicately over the bedroom window of Kalief Browder, a man who died by hanging himself from that same window at the age of twenty-two. On the morning of his death, Kalief told his brother that he was proud of him and checked to see if his mother, sat downstairs, was okay, before tying an air-conditioner cord around his neck and jumping from that window. When interviewed for a *Netflix* documentary about Browder's death and the events leading up to it his mother, Venida Browder, looked up at that bush and smiled. She said it reminded her of Kalief and his continued presence in their house and in her life. This ivy bush, which offers an eerie visual reminder of the cord that hung from that window announcing Kalief's death, told Venida that her son was still, in some way, living.

In the documentary, Venida expresses her reluctance to sell this family home. She explains that her hesitation stems not only from the fact that she raised all her children there, or that it was the place where Kalief died, but also from her attachment to the ivy bush. Not seeing that bush every day would mean risking feeling disconnected from Kalief and the comfort she associates with his haunting. For knowing onlookers today, this bush (if it still exists) might signify a macabre reminder of the suicide that took place in that house, for Venida it symbolized a life that was loved and prematurely lost because of state-sanctioned violence.

In May 2010, Kalief was walking home from a party in the Bronx near where he lived when he was stopped by police officers and accused of stealing a backpack. Kalief was brought to a nearby police station and assured that he would likely soon after return home. Unable to afford bail, Kalief did not return home but, instead, was detained in Riker's Island jail for nearly three years before he was eventually released. Roughly two of those years were spent in solitary confinement. Maintaining his innocence, Kalief denied the plea bargain he was offered on the condition that he admitted guilt for the offence. While he was imprisoned Kalief's accuser fled the country, which resulted in indefinite delays to his trial. After he was released from jail Kalief returned to his mother's home and made efforts to readjust to his old life. After finishing his high school education, he enrolled in Bronx Community College and made efforts to spend time with family and friends. As his story gained media traction, Kalief gave interviews on mainstream news outlets and appeared on national television.[1] During this time, he attempted to remain grounded in his home environment, one that had nurtured him but, ultimately, could not protect him from the brutal ordeal he subsequently endured.

In the neighbourhood where the Browder house stood greenery and access to nature were hard to come by. After his release from jail Kalief applied to a programme for formerly incarcerated people that would allow him to experience rock climbing, camping and other outdoor activities in Colorado, citing his need to get out of the city and experience a new environment to recover from jail-induced mental illness. Access to green space has proven health benefits, and for formerly incarcerated people (particularly those people who spent prolonged periods of their sentence in solitary confinement) it is often seen as a way to reconnect with a world that one has been excluded from. For many incarcerated people from inner-city neighbourhoods, access to green space is limited and, thus, not taken for granted. Due to limited exposure, green spaces are often idealized and imagined as symbolic alternatives to the concrete and constrained realities of urban life. During the Covid-19 pandemic, millions of people were temporarily exposed to what this reality might look like for the first time. People who did not have access to private outdoor space or who were shielding inside their homes because they feared catching the virus were routinely deprived of the green spaces that they formerly took for granted. For many, this deprivation signalled not only a loss of liberty but also a decline in mental and physical health. By temporarily unsettling the assumed accessibility of green space, Covid-19 lockdowns made clear the structural violence inherent in long-term confinement.

Prisons facilitate punishment by depriving inmates of their liberty and exposing them to conditions that human beings are not primed for. As social creatures, we are not meant to be involuntarily separated from our loved ones or to live behind bars. Nor are we meant to be deprived of the autonomy that would allow us to regulate our own eating behaviours, exercise patterns and social activities. Across the world, certain prisons are notorious for their severe and restrictive conditions. In 2023, the Centre for the Confinement of Terrorism (also known as CECOT) was opened in El Salvador as part of President Nayib Bukele's crackdown on gang violence. This maximum-security prison, which has capacity for up to forty thousand detainees, is a permanent home for inmates who are continuously deprived of natural sunlight, meat and outdoor exercise. Once they enter CECOT inmates have little hope of ever leaving, and because media access to CECOT is restricted it remains a prime site for potential human rights abuses. In the USA, jails and prisons[2] are, to varying degrees, sites of violence, terror and fear. For many inmates, the injuries they sustain while imprisoned extend beyond physical pain to include mental torture, particularly when their living conditions are squalid, physically restrictive and lacking in mental stimulation. This was Kalief's experience while coming into adulthood in Riker's Island jail. Physical violence was a

---

[1]   Notably, Kalief Browder appeared on US television show *The View* and developed a friendship with the TV host Rosie O'Donnell.

[2]   In the USA, jails are short-term facilities that typically house people awaiting trial, sentencing or serving brief sentences. Prisons are typically long-term facilities operated by state or federal governments for people convicted of serious crimes and serving lengthy custodial sentences.

daily occurrence, and severe mental ill health drove him to attempt suicide on at least five separate occasions.

In recent decades, growing evidence of the violence inherent in the US carceral system, along with increased awareness of how corporate investment sustains and profits from that system, has fuelled the rise of prison abolitionism. Led by prominent civil rights activists such as Angela Davis and Ruth Wilson Gilmore, the prison abolitionist movement critically examines the social and political conditions that drive mass incarceration and how they are shaped, motivated and governed by racist logics and beliefs. In doing so, it advocates for reimagining justice beyond punishment through imprisonment by envisioning alternative systems that do not perpetuate violence. Central to this movement's ethos is an understanding of 'the prison industrial complex' which, Davis notes, is a term 'introduced by activists and scholars to contest prevailing beliefs that increased levels of crime were the root cause of mounting prison populations. Instead, they argued, prison construction and the attendant drive to fill these new structures with human bodies have been driven by ideologies of racism and the pursuit of profit' (Davis 2003: 84).

Underfunded schooling systems, minimal job opportunities, inadequate housing and over-policing in Black communities are just some of the reasons why Black people are significantly more likely to be imprisoned or under correctional supervision than other groups in the USA. At the time of writing, despite making up roughly 14 per cent of the total US population Black people account for 41 per cent of the prison and jail population (Sawyer and Wagner 2025). This disparity, routinely dismissed as indicative of Black people's 'natural leniency towards crime', is, for prison abolitionists, a direct result of the disempowering social and political conditions Black people are commonly subjected to. The response to this crime should not be incarceration but increased investment to combat the conditions that generate it.

Prison abolitionists are routinely met with scepticism by critics who invariably perceive a causal link between crime, sentencing and incarceration. If a person is arrested, charged and found guilty of a crime, sceptics argue, they should be punished for that crime through appropriate legal means. More liberal sceptics might replace the term 'punish' with the term 'reform', with an emphasis on the need for rehabilitation to both take responsibility for, and work to change, their criminal tendencies, actions and/or behaviours. Yet punishment seems the most apt term to use when considering the multiple severe and inhumane practices that are a common part of day-to-day prison operations, such as solitary confinement. As I will discuss in this chapter, solitary confinement is one of a series of practices that influence rates of what medical practitioner and former chief medical officer of New York City jails Homer Venters terms 'prison-induced illnesses.' These practices contribute to a process of dehumanization that works to both discipline and degrade prisoners with the aim of transforming them into compliant and regulated citizens.

Those who maintain that there is a causal link between crime, sentencing and incarceration that justifies the use of prisons as mechanisms for punishment overlook the myriad ways in which people (particularly people of colour) come to enter the criminal justice system. As you read this chapter, thousands of people are sitting in US jails who are legally innocent and awaiting trial. Most of them are there because, like Kalief, they cannot financially afford to bail themselves out. Because of higher rates of arrest and poverty in Black and Brown communities these groups are disproportionately affected, resulting in an overrepresentation of people of colour who are legally innocent but nonetheless surveilled and penalized by the US criminal justice system (Alexander, 2010).

Kalief's story became a widely recognized symbol of injustice once it was made public. However, this acknowledged injustice did little to change public opinion about the positive correlation between arrest, detention and criminality when it comes to Black men. In this chapter, I argue that this is largely because of racist beliefs that render Black people in general, and Black men in particular, more likely to commit criminal offences than other racialized groups. Drawing on the successive waves of opposition to Black Lives Matter (BLM) protests from both right-wing and centrist critics following the movement's resurgence in 2020, I demonstrate how ideas of Black deviance and (un)deservedness are embedded in racist beliefs that justify heavier policing in Black communities and longer prison sentences. These narratives, I argue, preclude recognition of Black grievability by framing Black individuals as culpable in, and thus responsible for, their own suffering and death.

Cultural production of the 'Black criminal'

The cultural production of the 'Black criminal' speaks to grievability politics by placing negative perceptions of Black personhood in direct conversation with public assumptions about culpability and deservedness when it comes to the criminal justice system. In an ostensibly 'post-racial' era where racial discrimination is illegal (at least theoretically), the notion that any Western criminal justice system is permeated and/or shaped by racist logics and beliefs that disproportionately harm Black people is routinely dismissed as an absurd miscalculation. The prevailing myth that a disproportionate number of Black people are in jails and prisons through their own volition (i.e. because they have committed a crime that warrants state correction) serves to bolster post-racial beliefs in fairness and equitable treatment when it comes to state-sponsored punishment by assigning blame for that punishment, and any negative outcomes that result from it, squarely with the offender.

This myth not only overlooks the myriad ways in which Black arrest and detention are informed by racist logics that subconsciously (and sometimes consciously) presume culpability before it is known but also speaks to a wider cultural attitude of determined certainty when it comes to Black people 'paying the price' for their mistakes (whatever the cost). Black people who are incarcerated are often rendered ungrievable because they are understood to have precipitated their own fate, and that precipitation rests on prevailing beliefs about cultural susceptibility to crime and criminal behaviours within Black communities that inform wider social attitudes and beliefs.

In the critically acclaimed documentary *13th*, director Ava DuVernay maps the evolution of the 'Black criminal' as a culturally produced and cinematically reified figure who has been portrayed as a threat to White America since the abolition of US slavery in 1865. During the period of US Reconstruction, newly freed enslaved people were routinely viewed and problematized as a danger to ongoing systems that ensured Black subjugation in a well-established racial order that was created to bolster and uphold White supremacy. As a result, Black people were regularly controlled and forcefully governed by laws that ensured their subjugation by criminalizing minor offences and infractions that, if perpetrated by White people, typically went unpunished. These 'crimes' included loitering and vagrancy, both of which could be viewed as symptomatic of the socio-economic position that most Black people found themselves in at that time. Without recourse to public funds or federal assistance after they were declared free, many formerly enslaved people struggled to know how to proceed in relation to their newly granted freedom. How, many likely wondered, does one begin to form a life when that life has thus far been denied?

By criminalizing what are, arguably, symptoms of the material consequences of prolonged subjugation, laws that prompted Black criminalization rendered Black people blameworthy for their oppression by signalling their culpability in the 'crime' they were accused of. If they had not loitered, critics argued, they would not have been arrested and imprisoned. It was because of their individual actions, choices and behaviours that they were labelled 'criminals' and sent to prison. This conclusion not only takes for granted the legitimacy of laws that prohibit free movement but also highlights the importance of understanding the differential ways in which criminality is located and defined. To be labelled a criminal is to be positioned in opposition to the law and, consequently, to law-abiding citizens who operate within the legal frameworks governing day-to-day life. In other words, the term 'criminal' is a relational construct that works to separate individual dissenters from the compliant masses who, collectively, represent society 'as it should be.'

The application of the term 'criminal,' and its social salience as a marker of deviance and dissent, is largely dependent on how it is understood by the people and systems that give it meaning. On 26 January 1956, Dr Martin Luther King Jr. was first arrested by local police officers for offering car rides to people participating in the Montgomery Bus Boycott in Montgomery, Alabama (Maclin and Savarese 2018).[3] At this time and during his many subsequent arrests, King was legally branded a criminal and socially believed to be one by those who recognized his desegregation efforts as indicative of his opposition to existing legal structures. Today, King is largely memorialized as a national hero who brought about much-needed change through his social justice efforts. King's principles and actions remained the same during this shift, but the legal and social recognition of those actions as criminal or lawful changed in accordance with altered beliefs about the justification for a legalized racial caste system. King was ultimately able to transcend his 'criminal status' by changing ideas of what it means to be a criminal in accordance with local laws and customs.

---

[3] King was officially arrested for allegedly speeding but the arrest was widely seen as a pretext by authorities to intimidate boycott leaders.

Non-violence as a tactic of wilful non-compliance was used throughout the Civil Rights Movement to spur the elimination of a racial caste system that had legally relegated Black Americans to a position of second-class citizenship since slavery legally ended. Key to this tactic was the implementation of 'respectable' modes of dress, speech, and conduct that subverted stereotypical perceptions of Black behaviour and purposefully aligned individual actors with normative expectations of middle-class public comportment. Black and White anti-racist activists were seen and photographed sitting politely at public restaurant counters, reading or otherwise engaged in 'quiet' activities. Their peaceful demeanour stood in stark contrast to the unruly and often violent behaviour of White segregationists, who attempted to enforce the law by forcefully removing protestors from their seats, pouring liquids on them and shouting threats of violence to provoke a reaction. This juxtaposition was effective because it compelled onlookers to confront and ultimately dismantle their beliefs about what constitutes legal and illegal behaviour. Legally, the Black non-violent protestors were criminals for defying segregation laws by sitting in a 'whites only' area. Yet their peaceful *inaction* exposed the White segregationists' violent *reactions*, making the true wrongdoing more apparent in the aggressors' conduct. Knowing their actions would likely result in jail time, civil rights activists deliberately employed this tactic to provoke national awareness of the moral injustice in imprisoning peaceful people who pose no threat to the public. By silently placing their bodies on the line, these activists exposed the ethical contradictions of a system that punished non-violent resistance while allowing racist abuse.

In her book *The New Jim Crow: Mass Incarceration in the Age of Colorblindness*, Michelle Alexander unpacks this contradiction by considering how the presumption of criminality is inextricably tied to Black existence. 'Slavery defined what it meant to be black (a slave),' Alexander writes, 'and Jim Crow defined what it meant to be black (a second-class citizen). Today mass incarceration defines the meaning of blackness in America; black people, especially black men, are criminals. That is what it means to be black' (Alexander, 2010: 197). The mutually implicative labelling of 'Black' and 'criminal' points to an underlying assumption of an inherited predisposition towards criminal activity – one that renders Black people (and particularly Black men) a perceived threat to others' safety.

Stereotypes and assumptions about inherent Black criminality can act as political capital for politicians who purposefully invest in this image to publicly assert their opposition to it and, in doing so, gain political support. During his 1988 presidential campaign, Republican candidate George W. Bush publicized the criminal activities of Willie Horton, a Black man who stabbed a man and sexually assaulted his girlfriend while on permitted leave from prison during his custodial sentence. Criticizing his political opponent, Democratic Governor Michael Dukakis, for his support of permitted leave for incarcerated people, Bush utilized this image to affirm his position as the 'tough on crime' candidate and, in doing so, gained support from voters who were primarily concerned about reducing crime rates and protecting 'innocent people' from 'lawless offenders' through use of the criminal justice system.[4] By directly tying

---

[4] Here I put the terms 'innocent civilians' and 'lawless offender' in quotation marks to note their subjectivity.

Willie Horton's image to his violent offences, Bush stoked racial fears by evoking a national and historically rooted symbol of Black male violence to gain political support and affirm his position as a candidate who would keep (White) America safe by not allowing future offences like this to take place. Not only did Bush make clear that he opposed the scheme that enabled Horton to commit these crimes; he also voiced his support for the death penalty for first-degree murderers. In doing so, Bush positioned himself as the antidote to the 'threat' of Black violence by demonstrating his willingness to go to any length necessary to eliminate the national 'problem' of the Black offender.

This 'problem' is understood in relation to Black people more broadly because of how they have been routinely positioned as either culpable in, or imminently capable of, crime. As noted by philosopher George Yancy,

> Black bodies are constituted through a racist episteme, a way of 'knowing' in advance. Black bodies are shot not necessarily in exchange for what they do, but for what they will do. What they will do is based upon racial and racist teleological assumptions about the Black body itself, a body that is 'criminal,' 'scary,' 'demonic.'
>
> (Yancy 2017: xv)

By highlighting the positionality of Black bodies in the prevailing racist episteme as always being on the cusp of imminent crime, Yancy points to ways of 'knowing' that obstruct any understanding of individual culpability or responsibility. Because Black people are routinely viewed as a 'collective' in accordance with racist logics that promote ideas of sameness when it comes to behavioural traits and actions, their perceived threat to White people lies in their indistinguishability from the masses that are culturally recognized as violent offenders. This belief is largely driven by media representations that disproportionately detail rates of Black violence and anti-social behaviour (for example, looting) on television and other popular broadcasting mediums.

Being viewed as part of a collective rather than as an individual can generate negative feelings among those who internalize negative stereotypes about Black behaviour and subsequently question their own individual worth and future potential. This questioning can, in turn, constitute a form of symbolic violence that inculcates the oppressed person in their own oppression by causing them to propagate the very narratives that shape and reinforce their subjection. As a felt experience of one's subjection, symbolic violence can generate harm beyond a person's individual experience of it if the propagation that ensues contributes to racist policies and forms of racism denial that, in turn, harm others.

In March 2021, the UK government released a report examining the existence of ongoing racial disparities in education, employment, crime, policing and health. The *Report of the Commission on Race and Ethnic Disparities* (commonly referred to as the 'Sewell Report') was carried out by ten people, nine of whom were from racial and ethnic minority backgrounds. The chair of this report, Tony Sewell, is, at the time of writing, the head of a charity that aims to encourage 'talented' Black and Minority Ethnic (BAME) students who wish to pursue careers in science, technology, engineering and mathematics. Sewell's investment in BAME attainment is, for his supporters, evidence of his anti-racist stance and commitment to reducing racial and ethnic inequities in key areas such as education. Yet this report's findings, and Sewell's subsequent televised justifications of these findings, suggest otherwise. The overarching finding of this report is that institutional racism in the UK does not exist, which not only refutes the unequivocal and well-documented fact that it does but also denies the experiences of British people who routinely face it in on an everyday basis.

In the opening forward to the report, Sewell argues that the persistent inequities that exist in the areas studied are the result of socio-economic differences, cultural issues and familial failings that disproportionately disadvantage some groups more than others. They are not, Sewell argues, the result of institutional and/or systemic racism. He writes,

> Put simply we no longer see a Britain where the system is deliberately rigged against ethnic minorities. The impediments and disparities do exist, they are varied, and ironically very few of them are directly to do with racism. Too often 'racism' is the catch-all explanation, and can be simply implicitly accepted rather than explicitly examined. The evidence shows that geography, family influence, socio-economic background, culture and religion have more significant impact on life chances than the existence of racism.
>
> (Commission on Race and Ethnic Disparities 2021: 8)

By pointing to what he perceives as the 'overuse' of the word racism when discussing persistent inequities that negatively impact everyday life for racial and ethnic minority groups, Sewell dismisses claims of structural disadvantage in favour of a narrative that centres individual agency and responsibility in existing disparities. Later, the authors signal the absence of individual- and community-level engagement in matters that, they believe, warrant local interventions rather than an increase in state investment. This shift directly evokes a form of respectability politics,[5] wherein issues and concerns that are largely evidenced as societal problems are treated as the result of personal failings and a need for greater individual effort and accountability. The perpetuation of this narrative constitutes a form of violence when it inevitably fails to address (and in many cases exacerbates) systems and structures that the person is routinely subjected to but cannot individually overcome. When it is driven by members of targeted communities, this narrative can be further understood to signal their internalization of a belief system that marks them, and people who look like them, as the key instigators of any issues that cause them harm. As I discuss in Chapter 4, this internalization can reinforce conservative claims of 'post-racial fairness,' which promote meritocracy as both an ideal and a reality. It can also be used to justify narratives that place blame on Black people for the behaviours leading to incarceration.

Although the words 'Black' and 'criminal' continue to be used synonymously in the media and in popular culture, efforts to 'rehumanize' Black incarcerated people in

---

[5]   By respectability politics I refer to the practice of marginalized groups adopting behaviours or values deemed acceptable by the dominant culture in an attempt to gain social acceptance and reduce discrimination.

ways that purposefully distance them from the negative stereotypes associated with imprisonment are becoming increasingly common. These rehumanizing efforts often seek to underscore Black singularity to counter popular beliefs of Black 'sameness' when it comes to crime rates and anti-social behaviour. In May 2023, I visited the Schomburg Center for Research in Black Culture in Harlem, New York City, which, at the time, had recently unveiled an exhibition titled *Marking Time: Art in the Age of Mass Incarceration*. This exhibition showcased the work of over seventy-five formerly and currently incarcerated artists, many of whom sought/seek solace in art while imprisoned as a means through which to reclaim the dignity, respect and individuality they lost when they became inmates. Walking into this exhibition, I was struck by the first and most prominent artwork, which covered several walls. This installation featured a series of sketched side-profile portraits of mostly Black and Latino inmates with facial expressions that ranged from curiosity to benevolence to indifference. While incarcerated, artist Mark Loughney allotted twenty-minutes to sketch each inmate's profile using the limited material resources available to him, and in doing so created a series of images that both confronted and countered prevailing stereotypes of aggression and deviance that are commonly associated with Black and Latino prisoners.

Through Loughney's intimate characterizations of his incarcerated peers, the observer is compelled to deconstruct any pre-existing ideas of sameness they might have previously had when envisioning the archetypal Black or Brown 'criminal.' Because each incarcerated person is depicted in a way that marks them as categorically unique, their individual experiences both within and outside the criminal justice system are evoked in ways that prompt the observer to recognize their separate identities and acknowledge their overarching humanity. These prisoners are, at least temporarily, seen and fully recognized as individual human beings with different life histories and experiences. By centring each incarcerated person's humanity through unique characterizations, Loughney allows his peers to speak directly to those mischaracterizations and redefine themselves in relation to their known singularity.

Similar attempts to defy negative Black stereotypes that suggest a synonymous relationship between Blackness (particularly Black maleness) and criminality have taken place in the UK. In 2018, Black British photographer Cephas Williams launched *56 Black Men*, a powerful portrait series featuring fifty-six Black men wearing black hoodies, each accompanied by a caption highlighting their professions and achievements. The project showcases a wide range of roles, including teachers, graphic designers, doctors, actors, politicians and creative artists. When asked during an interview about why he was motivated to create this project and the underlying messages he wanted to promote through it, Williams responded by noting the importance of countering negative public depictions of Black men as victims and/or perpetrators of violence. By focusing on the myriad positive contributions of Black men, Williams's artistic direction hinges on developing an inverted and holistic recognition of Black male existence that directly confronts the viewer's own underlying prejudices and assumptions about what it means to encounter a Black man wearing a hoodie. Unlike Loughney's emphasis on highlighting the idiosyncrasies of his incarcerated peers, Williams purposefully relies on visual uniformity to promote a message of solidarity in tackling the issue of mass misrepresentation. Staring directly at the viewer with a singular expression of defiance, each of the Black men depicted directly challenges the viewer to see them as a stereotypical 'Black criminal' in view of their blatant contradiction of this stereotype as shown through their listed credentials.

One of the Black men photographed, number fifty-five, is David Lammy who, at the time of writing, is the UK Secretary of State for Foreign, Commonwealth and Development Affairs. In a 2019 *Guardian* article, Lammy wrote detailing his involvement in, and support for, the project, he cites the 2012 killing of US teenager Trayvon Martin as evidence of the fact that hoodies have become 'a highly politicised and racialised item of apparel' (Lammy 2019) that can contribute to incidents of prejudice and violence and lead to Black death. Lammy further notes the importance of this project in its commitment to going 'beyond the simplistic mantra of "not all black people wear hoodies"' that 'positions the hoodie in contrast to success' by situating hoodies and success as synergistic. Simply put, because these men are successful *whilst wearing hoodies* they demonstrate that one can be both, and in doing so contradict prevalent assumptions that one cannot be. This framing speaks to the need to recognize Black male humanity in its entirety rather than recognizing it, either solely or primarily, in relation to prevailing negative stereotypes.

Beliefs about cultural susceptibility to criminal behaviour within Black communities are perpetuated across racial divides and are sometimes espoused by Black people, some of whom feed into the narrative of Black criminality by expressing open disdain for Black 'criminals.' These 'criminals' not only seemingly signify individual failure but are also understood to signify the collective failure of Black people who act in opposition to socially sanctioned norms and behaviours. When asked about his motivations for maintaining his innocence and refusing the multiple plea deals that were offered to him during his time in jail, Kalief Browder noted that, had he accepted a plea deal, no one would have listened to his story because they would have viewed and quickly dismissed him as a criminal. If he had been convicted, Kalief infers, he would have been prevented from garnering any support for the injustice he suffered as a victim of the New York criminal justice system because his proven innocence was instrumental to him gaining public sympathy and the requisite media attention he needed to make his story known.

This need to be publicly recognized as innocent ultimately meant that Kalief remained in jail for longer than he otherwise would have, which undoubtedly contributed to the myriad health conditions he experienced because of his incarceration. Additionally, it likely increased his risk of death by suicide by prolonging his exposure to harsh prison conditions. It also gave Kalief an opportunity to challenge common assumptions about Black criminality that adopt a 'guilty until proven innocent' perspective when it comes to Black incarcerated people. By publicly asserting his proven innocence, Kalief defied these logics and, in doing so, made that defiance applicable to other young Black men who are currently in jail awaiting trial who may also be innocent and suffering the same injustice. The coercive nature of the US criminal justice system as one that overwhelmingly relies on plea deals rather than fair trials to secure convictions means that it is necessary to re-think and re-evaluate the common assumption that there is a causal link between arrest, criminal conviction and detention.

The symbolic violence that arises when Black people perpetuate negative myths and stereotypes about Black 'criminals' is rooted in a respectability politics that dictates 'appropriate' ways of publicly and privately acting and being seen. These respectability politics further shape grievability logics by assigning value to people who behave in ways that align with socially sanctioned norms and inadvertently emphasize the need for Black people to *earn* their grievability through conformity and compliance with those norms in Western neoliberal contexts. Black men who wear hoodies, have a criminal record, speak using 'urban' vernacular or in other ways challenge common modes of decorum that centre normative (White) expectations in terms of physical presentation and conduct are routinely (and often intentionally) disadvantaged in systems and structures that expect and idealize physical and behavioural compliance. As an infrastructure routinely used to punish those who fail to comply, the criminal justice system can be understood in Foucauldian terms as a primary state-sponsored disciplinary apparatus that regulates Black people's behaviour through enforced conformity and de-personalization (Foucault 1995). It also operates as a significant contributor to poor health outcomes and premature death among Black people, who face heightened risks of multiple health conditions once entangled in the system.

Prison-induced illness and 'Prison-Attributable deaths'

In February 2022, *New York Times* journalist Adam Liptak released a story detailing the experiences of Dennis Wayne Hope, a US inmate who, at that point, had been in solitary confinement in a Texas prison for twenty-seven years (Liptak, 2022). Originally sentenced to eighty years in prison for a series of armed robberies in 1990, Hope was sent to solitary confinement following a two-month prison escape in 1994. During this escape, Hope committed other criminal offences, including armed robbery and car theft. The conditions of the solitary cell that he was subsequently housed in – one that was 'not much bigger than a king-size mattress' (Reinhart 2023) – afforded little room for exercise or recreational activity. This, in turn, led to numerous joint and muscular issues that, over time, led to a gradual decrease in his mobility. Deprived of external stimulation or social interaction, Hope experienced a range of chronic illnesses that were directly caused by the conditions of his confinement, including depression, anxiety, paranoia, auditory and visual hallucinations, and suicidal ideation. The 'liberties' that Hope was afforded during this time extended to one hour of solitary exercise per day and one personal phone call when his mother died in 2013. His only human contact during the twenty-seven years he spent in solitary confinement was with prison guards, lawyers and, occasionally, journalists.

In a 2018 reflection piece on the punitive practice of solitary confinement, Supreme Court Justice Sonia Sotomayor notes that it 'imprints on those that it clutches a wide range of psychological scars' and, in design, experience, and application, 'comes perilously close to a penal tomb' (Supreme Court of the United States 2018). Through the use of the metaphor of a 'tomb', Sotomayor not only evokes the literal space that inmates are housed in but also the experience of living death that inmates are subjected to. Entombed in a space that signifies not only their exile from free society but also their separation from other inmates serving sentences in the prison's general population, people who experience solitary confinement (particularly people who experience it for extended periods of time) are at greater risk of injury from the conditions experienced by Hope and others that are linked to the mismanagement and/or neglect of chronic disease and self-harm.

Because it is indicative of a prisoner's short- and long-term health risks, solitary confinement should be understood as a key social determinant of health. According to the United Nations (UN), prolonged solitary confinement – defined as the confinement of prisoners for twenty-two hours or more a day without meaningful human contact for a period lasting longer than fifteen days – constitutes an act of torture (United Nations Office on Drugs and Crime 2015:13). The fifteen-day threshold marks the maximum period a person without underlying health conditions can endure absolute isolation. According to the UN, such measures should be prohibited for prisoners with mental or physical disabilities if their conditions would be worsened by isolation (United Nations Office on Drugs and Crime 2015: 14). With this knowledge in mind, it is important to scrutinize the ethical and legal rationales that are used to justify solitary confinement. It is also important to consider the extent to which these justifications depend on the perceived disposability of targeted inmates. When seeking answers to both, we might ask which types of behaviour warrant legalized torture? When prisoners are held in solitary confinement for non-violent offences, do the harms perpetrated *by* them outweigh the harms done *to* them? And given what we know about the significant health risks associated with solitary confinement (particularly for people with pre-existing health conditions), why is this practice sanctioned and upheld by a state that is ostensibly invested in promoting human life? In Hope's case, his solitary confinement was deemed necessary to prevent future prison escapes. Yet, Hope remained in solitary confinement for more than fifteen years after he was no longer deemed a flight risk – why? According to Liptak, the only plausible explanation for Hope's prolonged isolation was that it served as punishment for embarrassing prison officials by escaping and speaking publicly about his escape in televised interviews. If this is true, the torture that Hope was subjected to signifies an abuse of power from those officials who operated through the criminal justice system to enact personal revenge.

Incarcerated people from all racialized groups are subjected to solitary confinement and its harmful health effects. However, the disproportionate rate at which both are experienced by Black incarcerated people makes this practice a leading cause of racial health inequities in prisons. According to one study conducted in 2021 by researchers at Columbia University, one in nine Black men born in Pennsylvania in the late 1980s had been held in solitary confinement by the age of thirty-two for at least one day (Pullen-Blasnik, Simes and Western 2021). Of the Black men in this birth cohort who were incarcerated, almost 60 per cent had spent time in solitary confinement compared to 1.4 per cent of incarcerated White men in the same cohort. Additionally, close to 1 per cent of Black men in this cohort had been held in solitary confinement 'for at least a full consecutive year by age 32, compared to a cumulative risk of 0.2% for Latino men and 0.08% for white men.' In other words, Black male Pennsylvanians in this birth cohort are not only significantly more likely than White and Latino men to be held in solitary confinement, but also to endure it for durations that exceed what the UN deems humane. This heightened exposure, in turn, increases their risk of developing severe health issues linked to solitary confinement.

While solitary confinement is a leading risk factor for poor health in jails and prisons, it is by no means the only risk factor. In his book detailing his experiences as the former chief medical officer for the NYC jail system, Homer Venters describes what he refers to as 'jail-attributable' deaths which, he argues, 'stem more from the jail setting than from the patients, including deaths from withdrawal, trauma, suicide, and diabetic ketoacidosis' (Venters 2019: 24). According to Venters, jail-attributable deaths typically represent one-quarter to one-third of all jail deaths and are directly caused by the physical and social conditions of the jails that inmates are housed in. These conditions typically include poor access to health-promoting resources such as ventilation, nutritious food and sanitary products as well as neglect and/or abuse from corrections officers. Together, these factors can not only contribute to the onset of illness but can also worsen existing health conditions.

For some incarcerated people with life-threatening chronic illnesses, restricted access to medication and medical treatment creates significant barriers to effective care, often putting them at risk of premature death while in prison. When it comes to mental health care in Rikers Island jail, Venters found 'disturbing evidence that White patients were more likely to receive mental health treatment while in jail, while non-White patients were more prone to be punished with solitary confinement' (Venters 2019: 94). By positioning treatment and punishment as choice-driven responses to mental ill health, Venters demonstrates how racial disparities in mental health 'care' can be attributed to the decisions of individual prison officers who are able to wield their own biases. Ultimately, these decisions rest on the views and attitudes of people charged with maintaining order and enforcing compliance through detention protocols.

Research shows that incarceration-related health risks can extend beyond prisoners to include family members. According to one study conducted in the USA, family members of incarcerated people can expect to live a life that is, on average, '2.6 years shorter than that of [incarcerated] peers who have not been separated from siblings, children, fathers, or mothers' (Reinhart 2023: 560). According to the non-profit organization *Prison Policy Initiative*, roughly 45 per cent of the US population has a family member who has been incarcerated (Prison Policy Initiative 2023). If just below half of the US population has a family member who has been incarcerated, and this association is known to decrease life expectancy, mass incarceration should be understood and treated as a key public health concern.

Kalief Browder spent roughly two years in solitary confinement while he was an inmate at Rikers Island jail. During this time and in the years following his release, Kalief experienced numerous mental health issues that are directly associated with prolonged exposure to solitary confinement, including paranoia, depression and suicidal ideation. While enduring the health effects of prolonged isolation, Kalief was routinely denied food and showers by prison officers. He was also routinely mocked by officers in ways that worsened his mental ill health. According to a deposition Kalief gave two years after his release, during his first suicide attempt officers stood outside his cell and watched as he fashioned a noose and threaded it through his ceiling ventilator. After he tied the noose around his neck officers told him to 'go ahead and jump' before eventually entering Kalief's cell to remove him after he decided not to go through with it. In a 2016 article published by *The New Yorker* detailing Kalief's experiences in solitary confinement, Jennifer Gonnerman notes that in 'Rikers [Island jail], suicide attempts are sometimes referred to as "manipulative gestures"; at times, officers view them as efforts by inmates to escape from solitary confinement by faking the symptoms of a serious mental illness' (Gonnerman 2016).

Kalief's repeated exposure to the cruelties inherent in solitary confinement, coupled with the sadistic treatment he received from numerous prison officers, resulted in a death caused by state-sanctioned violence. Kalief's death, in turn, reflects a broader biopolitical project of disposability that renders the harm directed towards him meaningless (and, for the officers involved, seemingly entertaining) when understood within the confines of the criminal justice system. If that system had recognized Kalief as a human being worthy of respect, dignity and good health he would not have been incarcerated pre-trial for the length of time that he was. Kalief would also not have been subjected to prolonged periods in solitary confinement or encouraged to attempt suicide by watching officers who chose not to intervene until he later changed his mind. Kalief's dehumanization within the criminal justice system was necessary to create the conditions for this abuse to take place, and it was made possible by a criminal justice system that is structured to prioritize compliance with existing regulations over individual health and well-being. As 'one of many,' Kalief was viewed by prison officers as an inmate who needed disciplining rather than as a person who needed help.

When reflecting on the various social determinants of health that are generated through prison conditions, Venters points to data showing that 'a significant percentage of deaths behind bars are preventable' and suggests that 'we should treat incarceration as a risk factor for death, just like smoking or obesity' (Venters 2019: 26). People are arrested and incarcerated by state officials who have been granted the legal authority to detain them, which means their detention is upheld by a legal system that legitimizes their arrest and subsequent incarceration. If incarceration can be understood as a risk factor for death, it follows that the state can be understood as imposers of that risk factor. In this way, one could argue that the state is (at least in part) responsible for, and therefore culpable in, the prison deaths that occur because of poor prison conditions.

This framing is often refuted and recalibrated by conservative critics who argue that incarcerated people choose to commit crimes that lead to their incarceration. This view is widely refuted, both by prison abolitionists who view incarceration as an illegitimate response to crime regardless of the nature of the offence and by data that dismantles this causal link. According to research conducted by the Vera Institute (a social justice organization committed to ending mass incarceration), roughly two-thirds of the more than 740,000 people currently held in local jails across the USA have not been convicted of a crime. In 2021, the US Commission on Civil Rights released a report stating that more than 60 per cent of (legally innocent) defendants are detained pre-trial because they cannot afford to bail themselves out (U.S. Commission on Civil Rights 2022). The law that permits the (often indefinite) pre-trial detention of inmates who cannot afford to pay the required bail fee and releases those who *can* pay penalizes poorer people by default.

In 2019, researchers at the Federal Reserve Bank of St. Louis found that the median White family in the USA had $184,000 in accumulated wealth compared to $38,000 for the median Hispanic family and $28,000 for the median Black family (U.S. Department of the Treasury 2022). Equally startling is a recent statistic published by the National Bureau of Economic Research showing that, in 2019, Black Americans held on average seventeen cents for every White dollar of wealth (Derenoncourt, Kim, Kuhn and Schularick 2022). This economic disparity demonstrates an ongoing legacy of uneven wealth distribution that has disadvantaged Black and Brown populations since the US's founding. It also offers a useful framework through which to understand the various factors contributing to disproportionately high rates of incarceration among racially minoritized groups. Not only are Black people significantly more likely to be arrested for suspected criminal offences than White people, they are also significantly less likely to be able to pay for their bail release when presented with that option. In other words, because of the US's racial wealth gap, Black people are more likely to be imprisoned before being found guilty of an offence because they and/or their family members do not have the financial capital to bail them out of jail. This, in turn, means that Black people are more likely to experience the harsh conditions of incarceration for longer periods of time, and are therefore more likely to experience prison-induced poor health.

If the state is disproportionately imprisoning Black people and subjecting them to punitive practices that negatively impact their health at higher rates than other racialized groups, it follows that it is disproportionately subjecting Black people to risk of serious illness and death. This positioning reflects a contemporary form of biopolitics that allows (wealthy) White people to live and permits (poor) Black people to die by allowing the former respite from a system that causes ill health while subjecting the latter to it. The relative disposability of Kalief Browder's life serves as an example of this state-sanctioned biopolitics. Kalief should not have been arrested and detained for the crime he was accused of and, once arrested, his release should not have been conditional based on his financial circumstances. The fact that it was meant that Kalief was unduly subjected to the prison-induced health conditions that led to his death following his release.

Incarceration and physical proximity: kinship ties and social ex-communication

In the USA, detention sites are typically located in remote rural areas, far from the incarcerated person's home, family and community. Because of this, the inmate's family members and friends are often required to travel long distances to visit them, often at considerable financial cost. One could argue that the sheer scale of prison and jail infrastructure necessitates their construction in sparsely populated rural areas. Given that each facility often houses thousands of inmates, the expansive nature of these sites demands locations capable of supporting not only large inmate populations but also extensive staffing, including correctional officers, healthcare professionals and catering personnel. However, a more sceptical perspective might view the resulting social disconnection as a calculated motive behind placing prisons in remote regions. The remoteness of these prisons can facilitate the social disappearance of incarcerated people, isolating them from vital support networks, potentially complicating their reintegration into society, and diminishing public awareness of their conditions and experiences.

The physical distance between the average US prison or jail and neighbouring residential areas means that incarcerated people largely exist outside the purview of public consciousness. Because they are out of sight, incarcerated people are often out of mind, perceived as a distant collective rather than as individuals who had a life before they were arrested. The struggles incarcerated people face while in prison rarely enter public consciousness and inmates are often viewed as ungrievable by those who do not see them. As noted by Corrie Boudreaux in their research on public memorialization and grievability politics,

> one way that we abandon a life and make it ungrievable is by viewing it as irrelevant, by maintaining our physical and social distance. Because it is outside the borders of our social interactions, its existence does not affect us, nor do we affect it. We never knew it existed to begin with; therefore its loss is not a loss at all.
>
> (Boudreaux 2016: 410)

The failure to recognize individual loss as meaningful when it involves incarcerated people arguably stems from our physical and ontological separation from prisoners. Their lives are either seen as mattering less than those we regularly encounter or as 'non-lives' because they exist beyond our everyday awareness. Their physical distance and social absence can facilitate public apathy, which rationalizes our collective failure to recognize and act on the daily health risks that incarceration poses to inmates. In this way, visibility can be understood as a determining factor of grievability because of its role in making individual lives known and (sometimes) cared about. Visibility provides the groundwork for public empathy by making suffering both perceptible and relatable, and this can facilitate action when the person in question is recognized as a wronged recipient of state violence or as a person who is justly in need of assistance.

To be grievable, a person needs to be made known, and when that person is made known they need to be seen to matter. This mattering is often contingent upon that person's perceived social, economic or (in some cases) political contributions. The routine dismissal of incarcerated people as 'criminals' implies that their own actions led to the hostile living conditions they endure. This perception reinforces their vulnerability to being viewed as ungrievable, as it establishes a causal link between their actions and the state-sanctioned punishment(s) they face. When it comes to racially minoritized groups, ideas of culpability can be (and often are) further reiterated through racist stereotypes and imaginings. Scholar and activist Dorothy Roberts discusses this relationality in the context of Black motherhood, noting how Black mothers have routinely been understood as responsible for reproducing 'inferior traits' and 'deviant susceptibilities' in their children. This, Roberts argues, is often perceived as the root cause of contemporary racial inequities. She writes,

> For three centuries, Black mothers have been thought to pass down to their offspring the traits that marked them as inferior to any white person. Along with this biological impairment, it is believed that Black mothers transfer a deviant lifestyle to their children that dooms each succeeding generation to a life of poverty, delinquency, and despair … Disparaging stereotypes of Black people all proclaim a common message: it is the depraved, self-perpetuating character of Blacks themselves that leads to their inferior social status.
>
> (Roberts 1999)

By critiquing the centring of responsibility for Black poverty in Black mothers/motherhood, Roberts points to the injustice of viewing a systemic issue as a matter of individual culpability rather than an issue generated by broader forms of state violence and apathy. She further signals the perceived inevitability of Black failure by noting how this perception is tied to ideas of race as inherited and therefore biological rather than socially assigned. This idea – rooted in the need to justify racist action by attributing perceived racial inferiority to biology – is, in this context, presented as a key factor in Black ungrievability within neoliberal systems that equate human worth with economic value. Because Black mothers are seen to pass 'undesirable' traits on to their children, blaming them when their children do not succeed in life through traditional social and economic routes relieves the state of responsibility for persistent levels of racial inequity. As such, ideas of biological transference offer a scapegoat for states and institutions that generate forms of violence that perpetuate these inequities.

Routine barriers to employment, housing, health insurance and social security after prison make it more difficult for formerly incarcerated people to 'earn' their grievability through neoliberal ideals of hard work and self-determination. Branded as 'criminals' and either presumed capable of reoffending or inherently predisposed to crime, they often remain unseen even when physically present and materially known. In this way, incarceration functions as a system that further constricts grievability for racially marginalized groups by compounding the conditions that render them socially invisible. Posthumous grievability, a term I use throughout this book, describes how grievability can be selectively assigned after death, bringing visibility to those who were unseen in life. This occurs when individuals were positioned outside mainstream public consciousness, only to be recognized in death. This form of grievability is largely contingent on narratives that celebrate the individual achievements of the person who has died, and in doing so publicly recognizes their value and contribution. After Kalief's death, social and political commentators routinely foregrounded his academic achievements following his release from jail, framing them as evidence of his commendable resilience and determination despite his terrifying ordeal. While it is important to recognize Kalief's achievements and ambitions in life, centring the value of his life around both risks reducing his life to what he accomplished and intended to accomplish rather than its innate human value. In other words, rather than recognizing his innate human value, these narratives risk essentializing Kalief's life as one that was rooted in conventional recognitions of achievement.

There are vital lessons to be learned from experiences like Kalief's. The brutality that he endured during some of the most formative years of his life, and the ways in which that exposure brought about the shortening of his life, should be at the forefront of public consciousness when analysing this case. Importantly, Kalief's experiences should serve as evidence of why penal violence needs to end. They can also be used as a springboard to imagine alternative systems and non-violent futures that prioritize restoration over punishment and dignity over degradation. Through this consideration, I am reminded of a provocation offered by Christina Sharpe when reflecting on the everyday forms of violence Black people are subjected to – 'perhaps brutality enables one to recognise what tenderness is' (Loophole of Retreat: Venice 2023). In bearing witness to Kalief's story, we are called to challenge the structures that render such suffering inevitable for some and to envision a world where justice is not rooted in retribution, but in care and repair.

References

Alexander, M. (2010), *The New Jim Crow: Mass Incarceration in the Age of Colorblindness*. New Press.

Boudreaux, C. (2016), 'Public Memorialization and the Grievability of Victims in Ciudad Juárez', *Social Research*, 83 (2): 391–417.

Commission on Race and Ethnic Disparities (2021), https://www.gov.uk/government/publications/the-report-of-the-commission-on-race-and-ethnic-disparities (accessed 21 September 2024).

Davis, A. (2003), *Are Prisons Obsolete?* Seven Stories Press.

Derenoncourt, E., C. H. Kim, M. Kuhn and M. Schularick. (2022), 'Wealth of Two Nations: The U.S. Racial Wealth Gap, 1860-2020', *National Bureau of Economic Research*, https://www.nber.org/papers/w30101 (accessed 21 September 2024).

Foucault, M. (1995), *Discipline and Punish: The Birth of the Prison*. Vintage Books.

Gonnerman, K. (2016), 'Kalief Browder Learned How To Commit Suicide On Rikers', *The New Yorker*, https://www.newyorker.com/news/news-desk/kalief-browder-learned-how-to-commit-suicide-on-rikers (accessed 21 September 2024).

Lammy, D. (2019), 'David Lammy on Why There's Nothing Scary about a Black Man in a Hoodie', *The Guardian*, https://www.theguardian.com/world/2019/feb/13/david-lammy-on-why-theres-nothing-scary-about-a-black-man-in-a-hoodie (accessed 21 September 2024).

Liptak, A. (2022), '27 Years in Solitary Confinement, Then Another Plea for Help in Texas', *New York Times*, https://www.nytimes.com/2022/02/14/us/supreme-court-solitary-confinement.html (accessed December 19, 2025).

Loophole of Retreat: Venice. (2023), 'Christina Sharpe, Loophole of Retreat: Venice', https://www.youtube.com/watch?v=jdFilbViFN8 (accessed 21 September 2024).

Maclin, T. and M. Savarese. (2018), 'Martin Luther King Jr. And Pretext Stops (And Arrests): Reflections on How Far We Have Not Come Fifty Years Later', *University of Memphis Law Review*, 49 (1): 43–76.

Prison Policy Initiative. (2023), 'New Report Mass Incarceration: The Whole Pie 2023 Shows that as the Pandemic Subsides, Criminal Legal System Returning to "Business as Usual"', https://www.prisonpolicy.org/blog/2023/03/14/whole_pie_2023/#:~:text=At%20least%20113%20million%20adults,millions%20of%20people%20every%20day (accessed 21 September 2023).

Pullen-Blasnik, H., J. T. Simes and B. Western. (2021), 'The Population Prevalence of Solitary Confinement', *Science Advances*, 7 (48): eabj1928–eabj1928.

Reinhart, E. (2023), 'Reconstructive Justice – Public Health Policy to End Mass Incarceration', *The New England Journal of Medicine*, 388 (6): 559–64.

Roberts, D. (1999), *Killing the Black Body: Race, Reproduction, and the Meaning of Liberty*. Vintage.

Sawyer, W. and P. Wagner. (2025), 'Mass Incarceration: The Whole Pie', https://www.prisonpolicy.org/reports/pie2025.html (accessed 28 July 2025).

Supreme Court of the United States. (2018), 'Statement of Justice Sotomayor', https://s3.documentcloud.org/documents/4999298/Sotomayor-Apodaca-amp-Lowe.pdf (accessed 30 August 2023).

United Nations Office on Drugs and Crime. (2015), 'The United Nations Standard Minimum Rules for the Treatment of Prisoners (the Nelson Mandela Rules)', https://www.unodc.org/documents/justice-and-prison-reform/Nelson_Mandela_Rules-E-ebook.pdf (accessed 20 August 2023).

U.S. Commission on Civil Rights. (2022), 'U.S. Commission on Civil Rights Releases Report: The Civil Rights Implications of Cash Bail', https://www.usccr.gov/news/2022/us-commission-civil-rights-releases-report-civil-rights-implications-cash-bail (accessed 21 September 2024).

U.S. Department of the Treasury. (2022), 'Racial Differences in Economic Security: The Racial Wealth Gap', https://home.treasury.gov/news/featured-stories/racial-differences-economic-security-racial-wealth-gap (accessed 21 September 2024).

Venters, H. (2019), *Life and Death in Rikers Island*. John Hopkins University Press.

Yancy, G. (2017), *Black Bodies, White Gazes: The Continuing Significance of Race in America*. Rowman & Littlefield.

3

Understanding Black Lives as Grievable Lives: Black Lives Matter and the Murder of George Floyd

In both the USA and the UK, the systemic and disproportionate killing of Black people by state authorities has a deep-rooted history. Because of this long history, it is often anticipated by the people it has historically affected. It is common for Black parents in both countries to initiate conversations with their children at an early age about what to do if they are stopped by police officers while carrying out everyday activities such as driving, walking or shopping. By having these conversations, many parents believe they are preparing their children for likely eventualities. It is a practice of premeditated knowing and knee-jerk protection, one that anticipates violence before that violence has occurred. It is also common for Black parents to harshly police their children's behaviour in private so that, when their children go out into the world, they are less likely to commit the same offence and experience harsher policing from state officials and/or civilian vigilantes. As a form of 'protection', this parental violence can be understood as a perverse demonstration of love through its aim of administering discipline to reduce the child's risk of serious injury or death from state officials who might have the legal authority to inflict both. For scholar and activist bell hooks, this understanding is troubling because violent acts inflict further harm and, therefore, cannot be understood to accurately signify love. 'When we understand love as the will to nurture our own and another's spiritual growth', hooks writes, 'it becomes clear that we cannot claim to love if we are hurtful and abusive. Love and abuse cannot coexist. Abuse and neglect are, by definition, the opposites of nurturance and care' (hooks 2018: 19–20).

While hooks's point offers a clear logical rationale, when understanding parental violence as an outcome of legacies of racial trauma the dichotomy between love and violence becomes somewhat murkier. Rather than viewing violence and parental love as oppositional, we might focus on identifying the root cause and true perpetrator of that violence. Is the parent solely responsible for the preparatory act of violence that harms their child, or is this violence a shared responsibility between parents, legislators, law officials and civilians who routinely threaten and injure Black lives? How can we meaningfully attend to the harms generated through violence when Black children are subjected to domestic harms to protect them from state-sponsored harms? And what toll do these harms – both domestic and state-sponsored – take on Black parents tasked with keeping their children safe?

Black parenting, under the constant shadow of state violence, is routinely shaped by the painful knowledge that Black children's lives are often seen as ungrievable. Black parents in predominantly White environments often experience stress and anxiety about their children's whereabouts and activities when they are old enough to leave home unaccompanied. This pervasive fear has been extensively explored through fictional narratives that highlight the emotional toll of racialized parenting. In the 2019 *Netflix* film *American Son*, Kendra, a Black mother, arrives at a police station to report her son missing, only to later discover that he was apprehended by police officers while out driving with friends (Leon 2019). Kendra's response will be familiar to many Black viewers. She is both terrified and desperate. Standing in front of a White police officer who interprets her panicked response as evidence of hostility and non-compliance, Kendra's stress becomes more palpable as time goes on because she believes her son to be in immediate danger. While many parents would be comforted by the fact that their missing child is not only no longer missing but also under the watchful eye of police officers, Kendra's stress is heightened by the fact that police officers have her son. The film's tragic conclusion reflects the grim reality that, for many Black children apprehended and detained by police officers, death remains an all-too-real possibility.

When George Floyd called out for his mother while lying under the knee of White police officer Derek Chauvin, his death forthcoming and imminent, critics questioned whether he was indeed calling out for his mother or whether he was calling out for his girlfriend whom he allegedly called 'mama.' This question gained traction amongst those who sought to discredit Floyd and recognized the power of his invocation. The rhetorical potency of Floyd's emotional plea for his mother – an innate and childlike response to abject fear and helplessness – provoked widespread empathy from those who, through this plea, recognized the full extent of his vulnerability. This primal cry, uttered in a moment of crisis, became a powerful symbol of helplessness in the face of imminent danger. Floyd's invocation of it as he lay dying seemed to reflect a painful awareness of the reality unfolding around him in real time. 'Mama,' Floyd cried, 'I'm through.'

This declaration spoke to both present and vicarious onlookers who witnessed Floyd's death and recognized it as a cataclysmic demonstration of the human effects of police terror. By invoking his mother in his final breaths, Floyd indirectly spoke to all Black mothers who witnessed his murder. 'I heard this black man had called out to his momma as he lay dying,' one mother wrote, 'and I too am a black mother. One of the ones since time immemorial who have to answer the sacred call. Who have to answer the call for the divine sisterhood of black mothers. Even when they are not our own, we are asked to bear witness' (O'Neal 2020). By invoking a recognition of joint motherhood, Floyd's final words generated a shared understanding of communal vulnerability to state violence that is rooted in anti-Blackness.

The multiple stressors associated with Black parenting pose a significant barrier to reproductive justice. According to activist and scholar Loretta Ross, reproductive justice 'is based on three interconnected states of human rights: (1) the right to have a child under the conditions of one's choosing; (2) the right not to have a child using birth control, abortion or abstinence; and (3) the right to parent a child in safe and healthy environments free from violence by individuals or the state' (Ross 2017: 290-1). In other words, reproductive justice is not simply limited to one's ability *not* to have a child if one decides not to but also includes one's right *to* have a child and to be able to parent that child in a safe and healthy environment. For Black parents who are deeply aware of the over-policing of their children and the ever-present threat of state violence, this third condition is fundamentally unmet. Christina Sharpe captures this reality when she asks: '[i]n the afterlives of partus sequitur ventrem what does, what can, mothering mean for Black women, for Black people? What kind of mother/ing is it if one must always be prepared with knowledge of the possibility of the violent and quotidian death of one's child?' (Sharpe 2016: 78).

A Black parent's instinctive knowledge of their child's vulnerability to violent attitudes, forces and systems that predate them arises from a broader cultural awareness of how Black lives are treated as ungrievable. In the USA, this awareness is rooted in a country founded on principles of equality which, paradoxically, extend life to some and deny it to others. These principles, embedded in the US Declaration of Independence, entitle citizens to 'Life, Liberty and the pursuit of Happiness' in accordance with 'certain unalienable Rights' bestowed on them by God. The timing of this document is, of course, ironic, given that it was signed in 1776, a time when slavery was a common practice.[1] Moreover, its irony extends beyond the circumstances of its original signing to include contemporary examples of state violence that actively oppose its core ethos. If Black people in the US were truly considered equal citizens, their lives would not be constantly imperilled by the disproportionate threat of state violence they face. Likewise, their liberty would not be under constant threat from their disproportionate risk of arrest and incarceration. Their pursuit of happiness would not be obstructed by the compounding effects of institutional, interpersonal and internalized racism.

When Black children reach adulthood, the fear of police harassment and violence often becomes a matter of self-regulation and personal vigilance. Both behaviours are often fuelled by an adherence to respectability politics, which attribute survival and socio-economic flourishing to self-comportment and practising 'appropriate' modes of conduct. Recognizing the need for, and enacting, vigilance and self-regulatory behaviours in public spaces when Black is often denounced as both irrational and illogical by right-wing conservatives who utilize a post-racial ethos of equality to suggest the fears they are predicated on are false. At the time of writing, the 2024 US Republican election campaign has demonstrated a renewed interest in denying systemic racism and promoting ideas of individual responsibility and self-sufficiency when it comes to economic, social and political disadvantage. While once these opinions would have primarily been expressed by White politicians with an investment in maintaining White supremacy, Black conservatives are increasingly becoming vocal about the need for Black accountability and self-sufficiency in 'private' matters that are seemingly outside the remit of state or government regulation.

---

[1]   Many of these original signatories were, in fact, slave owners.

The idea that the political gains made during the Civil Rights Movement have facilitated a level playing field when it comes to state policing and state violence overlooks the myriad ways in which inequities persist in conditions that are beyond individual control. Post-racial discourse prohibits advancements in racial justice by contradicting the need for targeted interventions through an insistence on individual action and accountability. Global calls for racial justice in the wake of Floyd's murder were predicated on the understanding that Floyd's socially assigned race, and what that signified to the arresting officers, created the conditions for his demise. If Floyd had not been Black, this logics argues, Chauvin's response would likely have been different, and Floyd might still be alive today.

In this chapter, I examine the international impact of Floyd's murder and the degree to which it shaped public perceptions on the relationship between grievability and anti-Black violence. In doing so, I explore how right-wing representations of Floyd's 'culpability' as a perceived criminal who was accosted by police officers for 'legitimate reasons' reveal the limits of grievability within the context of Black life. I further show how the global resurgence of Black Lives Matter (hereafter BLM) protests in response to Floyd's death demonstrates a commitment to recognizing Black lives as grievable in contexts where, historically, they have been seen as ungrievable. In doing so, I discuss the sustainability of the global impact of BLM by examining the media's role in promoting Black grievability by reporting on Black death in ways that highlight Black victimhood.

George Floyd's murder as a modern-day lynching

When I first learned of George Floyd's murder, I was alone at home in my flat in Oxford, England, grappling with the intense loneliness that often accompanied long stretches of isolation during the Covid-19 pandemic. Fixated by the video that was circulating on my social media news feed, I sat on the edge of my bed and wept. Morbidly transfixed, I watched the life of a man who could have been my father, brother or cousin wither away under the knee of a man who had a defiant look on his face. Derek Chauvin appeared utterly unmoved and unaffected by the brutality he was enacting or the crowd bearing witness to it. Like many people, my immediate feelings after watching this video were a mixture of hopelessness and despair. Videos of Black people dying at the hands of police officers had become all too familiar by this point and it was evident to me that they were embedded within the social fabric that facilitates anti-Black violence and subjection in countries like the USA and the UK. How, I wondered, does one take apart and reassemble this fabric when it keeps so many people warm, sheltered and protected?

After the initial wave of public grief and despair, many responses gave way to anger. For many people, one of the most haunting aspects of the footage was Chauvin's expression, which was marked by brazenness and an unapologetic assurance of the legitimacy of his actions. Such displays raise pressing questions. How can such acts of violence be carried out under the banner of legal authority? What powers have been granted to law enforcement officers that allow for such deadly force against those they are meant to protect? This type of anger, as Audre Lorde reminds us, can be constructive when channelled in ways that promote social justice. 'Every woman,' Lorde notes, 'has a well-stocked arsenal of anger potentially useful against those oppressions, personal and institutional, which brought that anger into being. Focused with precision it can become a powerful source of energy serving progress and change. And when I speak of change ... I am speaking of a basic and radical alteration in those assumptions underlining our lives' (Lorde 1987: 3).

Floyd's murder was not the first instance of police violence to be captured on video and widely circulated online. Since the rise of smartphones and social media, activists (particularly those on the political left) have used these tools to expose systemic racism and galvanize public support for anti-racist movements. However, Floyd's visceral pleas, visible distress and slow death – coupled with Chauvin's chilling indifference – sparked an unprecedented shift in public consciousness. The result was a wave of international condemnation and solidarity with Floyd, his family and the countless other Black Americans who have long been disproportionately brutalized by both vigilantes and state-appointed law enforcement officers.

BLM, a social justice movement founded in 2013 following the killing of Trayvon Martin and the subsequent acquittal of his killer George Zimmerman, experienced a global resurgence after Floyd's murder due to its longstanding efforts to expose anti-Black violence and demand justice for its victims. By spotlighting their humanity, BLM creates the conditions for victims to become grievable through a recognition of the racial injustice(s) that led to their death. Because Floyd was physically restrained and immobilized by the officers who accosted him, he was physically unable to resist arrest or injure the arresting officers. As a result of this realization, Floyd's death was widely understood as an outcome of undue force that was made possible because he was seen as both inherently dangerous and expendable by the police officers in question.[2]

Because it was witnessed by bystanders and circulated in real time on social media Floyd's murder was widely described as a 'modern-day lynching' – a reference to the racial terror lynchings of the postbellum US South that disproportionately targeted Black people. These lynchings sought to assert racial control through fear by offering examples of what could happen if Black people breached the invisible racial line that governed the parameters of their existence. According to a group of United Nations human rights experts speaking shortly after Floyd's murder,

> [t]he latest videos to surface showing white men chase, corner, and execute a young man who was out jogging, or showing an officer kneeling with his weight on a man's neck for eight minutes shock the conscience and evoke the very terror that the lynching regime in the United States was intended to inspire ... Given

---

[2] The coroner's report following Floyd's death primarily attributed it to police restraint and neck compression.

the track record of impunity for racial violence of this nature in the United States, Black people have good reason to fear for their lives.

(United Nations 2020)

By demonstrating a linear connection between previous lynchings carried out by ordinary members of the public and modern-day lynchings carried out by White police officers, the authors of this report qualify both sets of killings as racist spectacles of violent control that were (and are) sustained to legitimize, ensure and propagate the existing racial order. In this way, the initial state-sponsored 'legitimacy' of the encounter between Floyd and the arresting officers can be understood to parallel the socially sanctioned 'legitimacy' of the anti-Black violence enacted by White mobs during lynching spectacles. Because both visually, symbolically and metaphorically invoke an anti-Black investment in maintaining racial dominance through their reliance on notions of Black expendability, they are equivocal in their contribution to the social and political devaluation of Black life. This provocation not only contradicts claims of racial progress that would have us believe that the US is now 'post-racial' following the political gains of the mid-twentieth century (Bonilla-Silva 2006), but also suggests a troubling transition from socially sanctioned but legally disavowed racial violence to legalized racial violence that is carried out on behalf of the state. While lynching was once a socially sanctioned but technically illegal practice, modern-day lynching is enabled by a legal system that often permits (and at times legitimizes) police violence that results in Black deaths. In this way, the racial violence we see today through instances of police brutality can be understood as a symbolic regression in racial progress, whereby anti-Black violence is no longer merely tolerated but legally maintained, supported and upheld.

As a practice that was purposefully created to exert racial control over formerly enslaved people, lynching instilled fear in those who viewed it as an impetus for constant vigilance when interacting with, and existing in relation to, White people. Lynching was, in turn, legitimized by White Southerners through the racist assumption that Black freedom posed a threat to White life, both in terms of the believed sexual threat Black men posed to White women and the perceived economic threat of Black enterprise and liberation. Lynching was also deployed to maintain an existing racial code that necessitated Black deference when interacting with White people. Black people could be lynched for minor transgressions such as looking a White person in the eye when speaking, not stepping off the sidewalk when noticing a White person walking towards them, or 'talking back' to a White person after being humiliated or demeaned. In 1955, Emmett Till's murder gained notoriety for the seemingly innocuous nature of the incident that sparked it. While visiting relatives in Money, Mississippi, fourteen-year-old Till entered a local store with his cousins and purportedly wolf-whistled at Carolyn Bryant, the White female store owner, before leaving. Growing up in Chicago, Till had not been conditioned by Jim Crow customs as his cousins had and lacked the intuitive knowledge of the deadly consequences that violating the racial code could bring to young Black people in the South. Shortly thereafter Till was kidnapped, brutally beaten and shot by Roy Bryant (Carolyn's husband) and J. W. Milam (Roy Bryant's half-brother). His neck was tied to a large metal fan and his body was discarded in the Tallahatchie River.

When Till's body was recovered and transported back to Chicago his mother, Mamie Till, insisted on opening the sealed casket so that she could see her son. The horror of seeing Till's bloated body beaten beyond recognition spurred Mamie Till's decision to display Emmett's body in an open casket and contact media outlets so that they could take and distribute photographs of it and make his murder known. By revealing her son's mutilated body to the public, Mamie facilitated a communal grief that galvanized a renewed commitment to civil rights activism and prompted a national reckoning with issues of race-based citizenship and racialized perceptions of human value. How, viewers likely wondered, can Black freedom be considered fully realized when young people like Till are brutally murdered in ways that make clear the lethal consequences of Black subjugation?

By viewing Till's body, national audiences were forced to confront the brutal consequences of racial hatred – consequences that had, until then, largely been shaped and obscured by a White gaze. Historically, images of Black suffering, particularly lynching photographs, have been circulated by White audiences as symbols of dominance, often in the form of postcards proudly sent to friends and family, sometimes accompanied by racist captions or poems. Photographs of Till's mutilated corpse served a radically different purpose. They exposed and condemned the very gaze that once used such images to assert power, turning the spectacle into a form of protest. These images catalysed a shift in racial consciousness, particularly among Northern viewers who had often regarded Southern racism as distant, exceptional and disconnected from the racial injustices embedded in their own communities.

By making her son's body visible, Mamie Till insisted on his right to be grieved. This was a political act that directly challenged the racialized hierarchies that determine(d) whose lives are valued and whose deaths matter. In exposing Emmett's mutilated body to the public, Till disrupted dominant narratives that rendered Black life expendable, asserting instead that her son's life was loved, lost and worthy of collective mourning and outrage. Moreover, Till's insistence on making Emmett's body seen directly confronted a criminal justice system that, up until that point, had failed to convict or prosecute his murderers. As noted by scholar and poet Claudia Rankine,

> [Mamie Till's] refusal to keep private grief private allowed a body that meant nothing to the criminal justice system to stand as evidence … In refusing to look away from the flesh of our domestic murders, by insisting we look with her upon the dead, she reframed mourning as a method of acknowledgment that helped energise the civil rights movement in the 1950s and '60s.
>
> (Rankine 2015)

Mamie Till actively transformed Emmett's life from an ungrievable to a grievable one, and in doing so created the conditions for subsequent Black deaths to be mourned and recognized within a framework that necessitates public acknowledgement of their humanity outside the context of their killing. By 'insisting we look with her upon the dead' Mamie's actions also raised ethical questions about the moral implications of looking and the moral responsibility to look. What does it mean for Black audiences to bear witness to Till's brutalized body as so many did, and how might this visual consumption differ from the ways in which White audiences saw it? Should viewing Till's body be understood as a moral imperative and, if so, for whom?

These questions resurfaced in the aftermath of Floyd's murder as multiracial audiences bore witness to a 'modern-day lynching' disseminated widely across social media platforms. Global audiences watched in real time as Floyd's body slowly became lifeless under Chauvin's knee and were subsequently interpellated in the scene that led to his death. For many, this interpellation led to a decline in mental health and well-being at a time when both were already significantly compromised by the Covid-19 pandemic. In bearing witness, visual consumers formed a collective audience that helped drive efforts to ensure Floyd's killers were held accountable, signalling an unprecedented global shift in public consciousness around systemic racism. By turning the traditional lynching narrative on its head, the visual distribution of both Till's body and Floyd's murder generated commitments to, and advances in, racial justice that might not otherwise have occurred. In doing so, they made room for an acknowledgement of the need for posthumous grievability to reconceptualize the lives of the dead in relation to the lives of the living.

Posthumous grievability and vicarious trauma

Every year, the Moore's Ford Memorial Committee performs a re-enactment of a lynching that took place on the outskirts of Monroe, Georgia, in 1946. This lynching, carried out by a group of approximately twelve White men, was motivated by the stabbing of Barnette Hester (a White man) by Roger Malcolm (a Black man) following rumours that Hester had been sexually involved with Malcolm's wife. After roughly eleven days in jail, Malcolm was bailed out by Loy Harrison, a White local landowner, in exchange for the promise of labour until Malcolm repaid his debt. On their drive back to Harrison's farm the car they were travelling in was stopped and the four Black passengers – Roger Malcolm, Dorothy Malcolm (Roger's wife), George Dorsey (Dorothy's brother) and Mae Murray Dorsey (George's wife) – were dragged from it, bound together and fatally shot. Despite local knowledge of the perpetrators of this crime no one was ever convicted for it and, at the time of writing, this case remains unsolved.

The decision to annually re-enact this brutal lynching was not taken lightly. Prior to the first re-enactment in 2005, the founding committee members were polarized in their views on whether it should be attempted, with some arguing that it would be viscerally repellent and unlikely to promote much-needed communal reconciliation and others claiming that it was a necessary step towards achieving justice for the victims (Baker 2016). Because both the perpetrators and individuals with knowledge of their identities could still be alive, proponents argued that re-enacting the lynching might encourage witnesses to come forward with information that could potentially lead to prosecution. Additionally, proponents argued that, in giving visual life to the plights or those who were lynched, these re-enactments humanized people who were, at the time, perceived as non-human. This argument is supported by scholars documenting these performances who substantially differentiate between the spectacular and subjugating optics of lynching photographs and the humanistic and educational optics of lynching re-enactments. '[L]ynching photographs,' cultural scholar Megan Eatman argues, 'typically show only corpses, sometimes with lynchers posing alongside them as if they were trophies. The re-enactment refuses that reductive narrative' (Eatman 2017: 163). In other words, lynching photographs centre the perpetrators of the crime whereas lynching re-enactments centre the victims of the crime, shifting the gaze from one of White supremacy to one of anti-racist action and intent. This shift reifies Black grievability by pivoting the narrative around the people who were murdered rather than the people who committed the murder, centring their experience of racial violence.

When asked by media crew why they decided to take part in the re-enactment that year, White and Black actors had mixed responses. For some White actors, playing the part of the lynchers allowed them to make visible a form of evil that they did not personally identify with but knew was an integral part of the South's history. By participating in the lynching re-enactment and unveiling its horror, these White actors felt that they could actively work towards ensuring that it would never happen again. In this way, the lynching victims are not only recognized as grievable through a posthumous recognition of their brutal murder, but also through their ongoing significance beyond the liminal focus of their killing. For some Black actors, participation in these re-enactments meant both paying homage to the victims and educating others about the truth of what happened. By educating others, these actors were able to testify on behalf of the victims who could no longer speak for themselves. In this way, these re-enactments signify a posthumous recognition of grievability enacted through an embodied humanization of the victim's suffering. This practice often came at personal cost. When reflecting on their interactions with the actors before and after one of the re-enactments, journalist Peter Baker notes:

> Darrius Bradshaw, who played Roger Malcolm, told me that during rehearsals – which, he reminded me, consisted largely of older white men calling him 'nigger,' tying a noose around his neck, and pretending to shoot him repeatedly – he sometimes sank into depression, and sometimes flared into sudden fury. 'Then,' he said, 'later, out in the real world, I'd find myself back in those feelings, not even realising at first where they came from'.
>
> (Baker 2016)

Because he was subjected to racist language and violence during these performances, Bradshaw viscerally re-experienced a simulation of the original attack in ways that directly compromised his health and well-being. Through the embodied feeling that his performances evoked Bradshaw transitioned from an actor to an actor-subject that personally feels, and emotionally responds to, another's trauma. Bradshaw's experience of racial trauma, often conceptualized as vicarious or secondary racism, occurs when a person experiences indirect exposure to racism and/or prejudice that is directed at another person.[3] When experienced in relation to extreme violence or murder, vicarious racism can significantly compromise a person's health by activating stress response signals that, over time, can lead to stress-related illness.

Activation of the body's primary stress response system, the hypothalamic-pituitary-adrenal (HPA) axis, initiates a physiological response that prepares the person who perceives an impending threat to react accordingly. In situations of acute stress, activation of the HPA axis can prompt necessary action by physically preparing that person to engage with the threat by increasing blood flow to essential organs (i.e. the brain and lungs), increasing heart rate and dilating pupils to enable clearer long-distance vision (Reed and Raison 2016). When stress-elevation from the perceived threat is ongoing, this response can increase risk of multiple health outcomes including heart disease, stroke, cancer, metabolic diseases and suicidal ideation.[4] In addition to direct exposure to racism, research shows that merely *anticipating* racist encounters can increase one's risk of stress-related health conditions when constant. In their study on racial and ethnic disparities in hypertension prevalence, Margaret Hicken and colleagues found that racism-induced vigilance 'is an important determinant of hypertension in Blacks (and perhaps Hispanics) through the continual activation of the biological stress response systems (e.g. autonomic and [HPA] systems) characteristic of this type of anticipatory and perseverative stress' (Hicken et al. 2014: 122). Similarly, in their study on the health implications of stop and frisk policies for Black communities, Naa Oyo Kwate and Shatema Threadcraft found that vigilance, anticipatory stress 'and the repeated cognitive engagement of stressors is associated with a number of [health] outcomes including depressive symptoms, sleep difficulties, hypertension and poor psychological health' (Kwate and Threadcraft, 2017: 545). In this way, Bradshaw's post-performance reactions 'in the real world', and the depression and fury that being in this environment often generated, could be understood as symptomatic of his response to anticipatory stress.

In her book *In the Wake: On Blackness and Being*, Christina Sharpe discusses the harms of vicarious trauma when enacted through the bodies of Black people who are living 'in the wake' of legalized slavery and anti-Black subjugation. By living 'in the wake', Sharpe argues, Black people tasked with re-enacting trauma are positioned as both in conversation with, and subject to, the trauma that their re-enactment evokes, and thus experience harm as both real and imagined subjects. When describing this harm, Sharpe refers to a programme called 'Cradle2Grave' that is administered by

---

[3] For further reading, see Alyssa Cohen, Patricia O. Ekwueme, Kaitlyn Ann Sacotte, Laiba Bajwa, Shawnese Gilpin and Nia Heard-Garris. (2021), '"Melanincholy": A Qualitative Exploration of Youth Media Use, Vicarious Racism, and Perceptions of Health', *Journal of Adolescent Health*, 69 (2): 288–93.

[4] In their study on food insecurity and paediatric obesity, June Tester and colleagues found that activation of the HPA axis triggers a cascade of hormones that eventually leads to the release of cortisol. This cortisol then 'stimulates highly palatable food intake (e.g. processed foods high in fat and sugar), which can lead to excessive caloric intake', increasing obesity risk amongst children (Tester et al., 2020: 443). This, the authors note, disproportionately affects children from disadvantaged backgrounds who are more likely to experience chronic stressors that trigger this pathway.

Temple University Hospital in North Philadelphia. This programme seeks to reinscribe the reality of gun violence and death amongst groups of predominantly Black inner-city adolescents by re-imagining what this might physically look like through visual re-enactment. Sharpe uses a photo of this re-enactment to visually communicate what she alludes to as the violent exposure of young people to trauma, many of whom 'are already experiencing trauma *from their material, lived violence*' (Sharpe 2016: 88). Through vivid narration, Sharpe implicates the reader in a scene that reveals the child's vulnerability as both a victim of violence and a spectacle constructed for both immediate and mediated observers. 'How,' Sharpe asks, 'are we to understand trauma here? These young people's bodies are always already in the space of [the dead person's] body; it is not that step *into the hold* that requires imagination' (Sharpe 2016: 89).

Re-imagining and/or re-enacting Black death is often perceived as a necessary trauma when it comes to reckoning with the reality of Black (non)life. For afropessimists, this reality is foundational to modernity and makes clear the necessity of re-imagining an alternative system to assert and ensure Black grievability. For afrofuturists, this reality offers a gateway for re-imagining alternative futures that normalize and essentialize Black grievability. The physical and emotional costs of bearing this burden through re-enactment for people who are, in different ways, implicated in its legacy raise the question of who should be doing this work. Should Black people re-enact this violence and, in doing so, purposefully resituate themselves in relation to it and, if so, what does it mean to work towards eliminating violence through practises that reinscribe it?

Judith Butler partially reckons with this question through their assertion that '[w]hen any of us commit acts of violence, we are, in and through those acts, building a more violent world' (Butler 2021: 19). According to this provocation, violence enacted in response to violence undermines the professed motive of peace that often accompanies violent acts that are committed in the name of justice. In this way, when police officers justify acts of brutality by claiming they were necessary to apprehend or restrain a suspect, it is important to question how that violence is framed and understood as violence (or not). What is needed, according to Butler, is an ethic of non-violence grounded in a recognition of our interdependence.

Butler's framework does not fully account for the pedagogical value of simulated violence, particularly in the context of re-enactments that aim to provoke collective outrage and moral reckoning. Such performances can elicit visceral responses from audiences who may come to recognize the grievability of lives previously regarded as ungrievable. In this sense, re-enactment can function as a tool for social justice by rendering visible the violence that has historically been ignored or denied. Additionally, Butler's argument overlooks the perceived necessity of simulating violence to prevent its reoccurrence. While their call for non-violence is ethically persuasive, it risks dismissing the strategic role that violent representation can play in building social awareness, mobilizing action and preserving collective memory. In some contexts, confronting violence through its careful and intentional depiction may arguably be necessary to create a less violent world.

Notwithstanding these important omissions, Butler's assertion highlights how historical displays of anti-Black violence can perpetuate further harm when they are re-enacted through the bodies of Black people who continue to live in the wake of both legal and extralegal histories of racialized suffering. In working to assert the grievability of dead Black people through violent re-enactments of their killing, living Black people put their own health at risk through their vicarious exposure to trauma. Following Tricia Hersey's claim that 'rest is resistance' (Hersey 2022), perhaps there is an argument to be made that Black people should be encouraged to practise anti-racist activism in ways that prioritize rest and care as radical forms of defiance. When framed in this way, anti-racist activism could honour the need for posthumous grievability while also sustaining an ethic of non-violence by rejecting the retraumatizing effects that violent re-enactments can produce within Black communities.

Conservative responses to political mourning

As well as sparking international anti-racist activism on an unprecedented scale, George Floyd's murder prompted widescale backlash from conservative critics who argued that anti-racist activism is unnecessary in 'post-racial' contexts where equality is (ostensibly) afforded to all. This myth of post-racialism, often justified through evidence of anti-racist legal advances, maintains that Western democratic countries like the UK and the USA no longer purposefully and unfairly discriminate against racially minoritized groups and, therefore, cannot be understood as systemically or inherently racist. This liminal view of racism confines this practice to overt forms of discrimination that indisputably intend to harm, kill, humiliate, and/or disadvantage the targeted person or group through language and/ or direct action. In April 1993, when eighteen-year-old Stephen Lawrence was murdered in southeast London by a group of White youths, few questioned the racist motivations of his attackers who called out 'what, what nigger?' before stabbing him to death (Macpherson 1999). Similarly, when self-proclaimed White supremacist Dylan Roof fatally shot nine Black members of the Emanuel African Methodist Episcopal Church in Charleston, South Carolina in June 2015 to provoke a race war, few questioned whether his crime was racially motivated. Yet instances of racism that are communicated through coded language and actions that signify racist intent without directly stating that fact are routinely viewed as ambiguous, debatable or inconsequential by those who are persuaded by post-racial articulations of ostensible equality.

For the people who fall into this category, Floyd's murder was often seen as a tragic outcome of his own drug abuse and non-compliance. During a roundtable discussion on her self-titled podcast in July 2021, conservative commentator Candace Owens, perhaps one of the most outspoken critics of George Floyd and the Black Lives Matter movement, repeatedly cited Floyd's alleged fentanyl use prior to his arrest as evidence of his supposed criminality (Owens 2021). Owens used this claim to support her view that Floyd should not be memorialized as a symbol of social justice. Responding to arguments that Floyd's death made clear the continuation of anti-Black racism within US society and culture, Owens argued that Barack Obama 'would never have been president had it not been for the fact that America has moved on from race' and that the media and Democratic politicians 'don't want us to move on from race' because it upholds and promotes their own political agenda. By emphasizing Floyd's alleged criminal behaviour and denying that racial bias played a role in his death, Owens exemplifies a neoliberal conservative approach to state violence – one that centres individual actions and personal responsibility in assigning culpability. Her argument implies that, if Floyd had not ingested fentanyl or resisted arrest, he might still be alive today.

Owens is joined in this rationale by conservative political commentators like Brandon Tatum who, during this roundtable discussion, argued that Floyd was a 'thug', 'criminal' and drug user who should not serve as an example for anyone (Owens 2021). By defaming Floyd's character in the context of his killing, Tatum implies that only those who are law-abiding and who consistently embody idealized standards of behaviour are worthy of being mourned or celebrated. This reductive and limiting framework leaves little room for human error in cases that prompt public and political mourning. It also narrows the boundaries of grievability by reserving it for those whose posthumous legacy can be framed as a model for 'correct' ways of living.

I use the term political mourning to describe and attend to the framework that facilitates social justice in response to state-actioned violence against marginalized groups. In this way, political mourning highlights and reinforces the nature of this injustice whilst opening pathways for social and legal change to prevent its reoccurrence. Conservative responses to political mourning often express scepticism towards claims that systemic discrimination underlies state-sanctioned or state-promoted violence. In doing so, they push back against political mourning by arguing that social justice advocates frequently overlook the social, political and legal progress made towards achieving equality. In her book *Ecologies of Harm: Rhetorics of Violence in the United States*, Megan Eatman refutes conservative positionalities that centre progress by connecting overt forms of White supremacy to contemporary forms of anti-Black state violence. Referring to the high-profile killing of Black teenager Michael Brown by White police officer Darren Wilson in 2014, Eatman argues that '[u]nlike acts of terrorism or state-run execution, Brown's murder was not planned for persuasive effect' but nevertheless shared 'contagions and energy' with other forms of White supremacist rhetoric that circulate the underlying impetus of this history (Eatman 2020: 1–2). Responding to conservative efforts to deconstruct Brown's victimhood by pointing to alleged previous criminal misdeeds Eatman writes,

> By reiterating the topos that Brown was 'no angel' and highlighting his alleged criminal actions, distant rhetors constitute themselves, along with Wilson, as agents protecting racialized 'law-abiding citizens' from menacing 'thugs.' While Wilson never declared that he was 'sending a message' by shooting Brown, his actions reenergised existing white supremacist rhetoric, and the fallout from the murder offered additional opportunities for white supremacist identity formation.
>
> (Eatman 2020: 2)

In making this point, Eatman underscores the productive role of criminalization by constituting a distinction between the 'criminal Other' and the 'good citizen.' By positioning Brown as a criminal, Eatman infers, conservative commentators were more able to mobilize support for Wilson in his capacity as a person appointed by the state to protect 'law-abiding citizens' from 'menacing thugs.' As we saw in Chapter 2, this distinction is a necessary and inherent component of US mass incarceration, which is maintained (at least in part) by a belief in the causal sequence between individual action and individual outcomes.

By centring an ecology of harm in their exploration of anti-Black state violence, Eatman underscores how cultural violence that is expressed through language leads to the dehumanization of populations, which makes possible their killing with relative impunity. The relative disposability of dehumanized populations because of rhetoric that renders them vulnerable to and, in some cases, seemingly 'deserving of' their death reiterates the disjuncture between grievable and ungrievable lives by assigning human value to 'positive' and 'negative' lifestyle behaviours. By framing grievable lives as those of 'law-abiding citizens' and ungrievable lives as those of individuals who exhibit behaviours deemed antithetical to normative and respected forms of self-regulation, conservative critics effectively excuse (and in some cases support) state-sanctioned violence against demonized groups in the name of 'protecting the innocent.' Collectively, these 'innocent people' represent an idealized community that upholds and reinforces neoliberal models of 'good citizenship,' which perpetuate exclusions and disproportionately assign vulnerability to those who fail to meet their standards.

Cultural violence, a term Eatman uses to describe the cultural mechanisms that enable the dehumanization of certain populations, is often enacted through respectability politics. These politics complicate political framings of Black personhood by challenging stereotypical notions of Black 'deviance,' non-compliance and criminality with representations of Black achievement, success and self-determination. Candace Owens herself embodies this confrontation as a Black woman born into disadvantaged circumstances who subsequently became an entrepreneur and amassed a multi-million-dollar fortune. Conservative pushback against recognitions of anti-Black state violence operates as a form of cultural violence in ways that centre the performativity of language in constructing ideas of (non)personhood. Describing Floyd as a 'thug' and a 'criminal' lends credence to arguments that intend to persuade centrist and right-leaning critics of Floyd's culpability in his death, therein detracting from state culpability and the need for widescale reform and political mourning.

In modelling her success as an outcome of her hard work and determination, Owens reiterates a conservative ethos promoted by author and educator Booker T. Washington in the post-Reconstruction era that advances a 'pull yourself up by your bootstraps' approach to racial advancement and development. Incurring criticism from numerous prominent Black intellectuals at the time (perhaps most notably W. E. B Du Bois), Washington argued that racial uplift among Black people could be achieved only through vocational education and pragmatic entrepreneurship. Unlike many of his contemporaries, Washington argued that this advancement should happen gradually and advised against agitation to secure Black political freedoms (Washington 2018).

Critics argue that this approach to racial uplift re-entrenches modes of second-class citizenship that render Black people inferior and less deserving of state investment than their White counterparts. In this way, Washington's ethos can be understood as upholding a system of relative disposability that allows racialized perceptions of value to determine who is more or less likely to succeed in life. By advocating for Black self-determination within the constraints of second-class citizenship, Washington arguably overlooks the extent to which racial progress depends on a collective recognition of mutual dependency and a shared investment in racial equity and social justice. Such equity requires a mutual acknowledgement of equal human value, made visible through an understanding of interdependence. Washington's framework also limits the possibility of recognizing Black grievability, which relies on the social and political affirmation of equal worth. By insisting on racial uplift within a structurally unequal, two-tiered system, he inadvertently reinforces the very belief system that often renders Black lives ungrievable.

Black respectability politics centre individual agency, ambition and determination in lifestyle-related health outcomes, educational attainment, financial success and one's ability to attain and maintain a 'happy' life. By positioning choice as a determining factor in achieving 'happiness,' advocates commonly attribute blame to the individual who is believed to have caused their own unhappiness by making poor lifestyle choices. This liminal binary ('good choices' lead to a happy life, 'poor choices' lead to an unhappy life) creates a framework through which inter- and intra-racial differences in opportunity, income and poor lifestyle-related health outcomes are seen as avoidable realities that can (and should) be independently managed and prevented. This recognition, in turn, sustains (un)grievability by assigning value to those who make 'good choices' and withholding value from those who make 'poor choices'.

Although beliefs in post-racialism maintain a superficial recognition of equal human value, the structural conditions that routinely prevent racially minoritized groups from making 'good choices' and achieving 'happiness' are erased through this binary. As noted by Keisha Ray in her foregrounding of Black bioethics as a critical discipline,

> if the dominant story is that Black people are sick because of their own moral failings and not the failings of the institutions around them … then they [institutions] do not have to be held responsible for the damage they cause to Black people's health. Furthermore, if institutions are not held responsible for the ways they make Black people sick, then they do not have to change.
>
> (Ray et al. 2023: 254)

By framing structural conditions as individually blameworthy, advocates and practitioners of Black respectability politics divest responsibility from state actors and institutions that create and maintain these conditions and reallocate it to individuals who, by themselves, are prevented from generating meaningful change. This reallocation, in turn, feeds a broader narrative of blame and shame that stigmatizes dispossessed people for their failure to adhere to aspirational (yet normative) expectations.

Being posthumously understood as worthy of political mourning typically necessitates engagement in, and conformity to, some form of respectability politics.

For Black people, these politics often necessitate physical and/or verbal disengagement with racialized stereotypes that might otherwise render them unworthy/undeserving of public sympathy. Yet conformity to respectability politics does not necessarily shield Black people from harm. During his reflections on the limited protections afforded to Black individuals who embody respectability politics in everyday social interactions, US civil rights attorney and activist Bryan Stevenson recalled being stopped and harassed at gunpoint by police officers in Atlanta, Georgia, while preparing for an upcoming court case (NowThis Impact 2020). Even as a prominent attorney and a graduate of Harvard Law School, Stevenson found himself needing to pacify police officers and actively counteract their presumption that he represented a threat to public safety. '[A]ll of that hard work and education,' Stevenson notes, 'didn't shield me from that threat and violence.' From a humanitarian and ethical viewpoint, perceived respectability should not be a requirement of day-to-day living. Even when considered pragmatically – as a strategy that acknowledges its routine function despite its ethically contested foundation – respectability proves to be an inadequate safeguard against the structural realities of systemic racism. It is therefore necessary to interrogate *why* respectability continues to be promoted as a viable form of protection, and what ideological investments sustain the idea that it remains an accessible and effective choice for all.

References

American Son (2019), [Film] Dir. L. Leon, Netflix.

Baker, P. (2016), 'A lynching in Georgia: The Living Memorial of America's History of Racist Violence', *The Guardian*, https://www.theguardian.com/world/2016/nov/02/a-lynching-in-georgia-the-living-memorial-to-americas-history-of-racist-violence (accessed 19 September 2024).

Bonilla-Silva, E. (2006), *Racism without Racists: Color-Blind Racism and the Persistence of Racial Inequality in the United States.* Rowman & Littlefield.

Butler, J. (2021), *The Force of Non-Violence: An Ethico-Political Bind.* Verso.

Eatman, M. (2017), 'Loss and Lived Memory at the Moore's Ford Lynching Reenactment', *Advances in the History of Rhetoric*, 20 (2): 153–66.

Eatman, M. (2020), *Ecologies of Harm: Rhetorics of Violence in the United States.* Ohio State University Press.

Hersey, T. (2022), *Rest Is Resistance: Free Yourself from Grind Culture and Reclaim Your Life.* Aster.

Hicken, M. T., H. Lee, J. Morenoff, J. S. House and D. R. Williams. (2014), 'Racial/ Ethnic Disparities in Hypertension Prevalence: Reconsidering the Role of Chronic Stress', *American Journal of Public Health*, 104 (1): 117–23.

hooks, b. (2018), *All About Love: New Visions.* HarperCollins.

Kwate, O. A. and S. Threadcraft. (2017), 'Dying Fast and Dying Slow in Black Space: Stop and Frisk's Public Health Threat and a Comprehensive Necropolitics', *Du Bois Review*, 14 (2): 535–56.

Lorde, A. (1987), 'The Uses of Anger: Women Responding to Racism', *Women and Language*, 11 (1): 1–8.

Macpherson, W. (1999), 'The Stephen Lawrence Inquiry', https://assets.publishing.service. gov.uk/media/5a7c2af540f0b645ba3c7202/4262.pdf (accessed 22 September 2024).

NowThis Impact. (2020), '"Respectability Politics" Won't Protect Black Americans From Racism', https://www.youtube.com/watch?v=mfIlqoNcpDs (accessed 24 September 2024).

O'Neal, L. (2020), 'George Floyd's Mother was Not There, but He Used Her as a Sacred Invocation', *National Geographic*, https://www.nationalgeographic.com/history/article/ george-floyds-mother-not-there-he-used-her-as-sacred-invocation (accessed 22 September 2024).

Owens, C. (2021), 'CANDACE OWENS: George Floyd is NOT a Hero', https://www. youtube.com/watch?v=HVUGy8NVYsc (accessed 22 September 2024).

Rankine, C. (2015), 'The Condition of Black Life is One of Mourning', https://www. nytimes.com/2015/06/22/magazine/the-condition-of-black-life-is-one-of-mourning. html (accessed 22 September 2024).

Ray, K., F. E. Fletcher, D. O. Marteschenko and J. E. James. (2023), 'Black Bioethics in the Age of Black Lives Matter', *Journal of Medical Humanities*, 44 (2): 251–67.

Reed, R. G. and C. L. Raison. (2016), 'Stress and the Immune System'. In *Environmental Influences of the Immune System*, edited by C. Esser, pp. 97–126. Springer.

Ross, L. J. (2017), 'Reproductive Justice as Intersectional Feminist Activism', *Souls*, 19 (3): 286–94.

Sharpe, C. (2016), *In the Wake: On Blackness and Being*. Duke University Press.

Tester, J. M., L. G. Rosas and C. W. Leung. (2020), 'Food Insecurity and Pediatric Obesity: A Double Whammy in the Era of Covid-19', *Current Obesity Reports*, 9: 442–50.

United Nations. (2020), 'UN Experts Condemn Modern-day Racial Terror Lynchings in US and Call for Systemic Reform and Justice', https://www.ohchr.org/en/press-releases/2020/06/un-experts-condemn-modern-day-racial-terror-lynchings-us-and-call-systemic (accessed 20 September 2024).

Washington, B. (2018), *Up from Slavery*. Arcturus Publishing.

4

Ungrievability Unveiled: 'Jihadi Brides' and the Case of Shamima Begum

In February 2015, fifteen-year-old Shamima Begum, along with her school friends Amira Abase and Kadiza Sultana, left the UK to join the newly established Islamic State of Iraq and Syria (ISIS). After months of online grooming, careful planning and communication with ISIS affiliates already in Syria, the three girls boarded a flight from London to Istanbul. From there, they were smuggled across the Turkey–Syria border by a Canadian intelligence informant, who reportedly provided information on ISIS defectors to opposing authorities in exchange for the promise of Canadian citizenship (Baker 2022).

Initial news stories documenting the defection of the 'Bethnal Green schoolgirls,' as they were widely known, largely focused on the plight of their families who remained in Britain and the emotional toll it took on them. In televised appeals, relatives spoke of their shock and pointed to the London Metropolitan Police (Met Police) for failing to prevent their defections. Several months before Shamima, Amira and Kadiza left London, their fifteen-year-old schoolmate Sharmeena Begum also joined ISIS, presumably via a similar route. That earlier defection prompted a joint inquiry by the Met Police and Bethnal Green Academy (the girls' school) to determine how Sharmeena was able to leave and the underlying motivations behind this decision.

With permission from the school, the Met Police wrote a letter to the girls' parents informing them of what had happened and seeking permission to interview their daughters to shed further light on Sharmeena's disappearance. These letters were not directly delivered to their parents but, instead, were given to the girls to deliver, which meant that they were hidden from view and only found in the months following their departure. Had they been made aware of Sharmeena's disappearance, the parents argued, they would have strictly surveilled their children and their defection to ISIS would not have been possible (Dodd and Gani 2015).

Four years later, in February 2019, Shamima Begum was found heavily pregnant with her third child by UK war correspondent Anthony Loyd in al-Hol detention camp in northern Syria. When asked by Loyd about her experiences in ISIS during the four years she spent there and the circumstances leading up to her detention Begum replied by saying that, when she arrived in Raqqa,[1] it appeared as it had done in the propaganda videos she had seen before leaving Britain. When pressed about what she witnessed

---

[1] Raqqa was the primary/major city in Syria controlled and governed by ISIS.

during her time in ISIS Begum noted that she saw a beheaded head in a rubbish bin and that 'it didn't faze [her] at all' (The Times 2019). This admission, made quickly and with a tone of nonchalance, would be repeated over the course of subsequent years as evidence of Begum's unsuitability for repatriation to Britain.

Citing the health and safety of her unborn child as her primary motivation, Begum expressed her desire to return to the UK during her initial interview so that her son might receive NHS treatment, despite remaining unrepentant about her decision to join ISIS. In a subsequent interview shortly after her son Jarrah was born Begum reiterated this point, stating she had no regrets about joining ISIS before Raqqa fell to US-led coalition forces. She also said she was 'ok' with the acts of violence she witnessed and did not question them (Sky News 2019). Dazed and exhausted, Begum appeared on camera answering the journalist's questions in an unprepared and seemingly candid way, while an anonymous woman next to her wearing a niqab silently cradled her son, occasionally glancing in Begum's direction. Their eyes never met during the interview, and it is unclear whether they were trusted friends or untrusting enemies.

During the months following the public release of this interview, Begum's plea for repatriation gained increasing notoriety in the UK. Acrimonious attitudes were formed and widely shared on social media by members of the British public who saw her as a traitor who was undeserving of public sympathy or government assistance. Alongside Begum's growing notoriety came an awareness of how the conditions she was under while being interviewed by foreign journalists prevented Begum from speaking freely whilst on camera. Threats of violence against former ISIS supporters that were perceived to be speaking negatively about the 'caliphate'[2] were rife within the detention camp, and threats of tent burning in the middle of the night were common. Indeed, after she had been moved to the comparably safer but highly dangerous al-Roj camp, Begum repeatedly expressed her fear of 'the women' who posed a threat to anyone speaking out against ISIS and consistently surveilled media communication between camp detainees and Western journalists. Yet the vitriol that was directed towards Begum by the British public continued to increase and, at certain points, became ubiquitous, with social media influencers, political pundits and ordinary British citizens across the political spectrum expressing their disdain for Begum and pointedly rejecting her repeated requests for mercy.

In a BBC documentary released in February 2023, investigative journalist Joshua Baker shed further light on the practical details of Shamima Begum's defection to ISIS, including the route she took, a timeline of her experiences while there, and the circumstances leading up to her detection four years after leaving Britain. Upon entry into Raqqa, Shamima, Amira and Kadiza were sent to a local madafa where they, along with other unmarried girls and women, were forced to remain until they got married. Desperate to leave the overcrowded and unsanitary conditions of the madafa Shamima and her friends quickly married, each selecting English-speaking husbands who

---

[2] Note that the term 'caliphate' was commonly used among ISIS supporters who lived within its territories.

worked for, or under, ISIS. Amira married an eighteen-year-old Australian jihadist who was later killed in US-led coalition airstrikes and Kadiza married a Somalian-American man who died in a Russian airstrike in 2016. At the time of writing, Kadiza has been confirmed dead and Amira is believed to be dead.

Shamima married Yago Riedjik, a 21-year-old Dutch ISIS fighter, roughly three weeks after arriving in Raqqa. Throughout this documentary, the coercive and abusive nature of their relationship and the circumstances that instigated it are made clear, and particular attention is paid to their difference in age and the expectations of marriage under ISIS rule. Describing her decision to get married as comparable to prostitution, Begum details how she felt forced to marry to leave the dire conditions of the madafa. She further describes how her relationship with her husband, while initially amicable, quickly became violent and abusive after he was released from jail where he spent seven months on suspicion of spying. After his release, Shamima subsequently gave birth to three children in quick succession, all of whom died from malnutrition and respiratory illnesses whilst in her care.[3]

Begum's third child, whom she named Jarrah after her first son, was just under three-weeks-old when he died from pneumonia. The noxious conditions of the detention camp he was housed in, coupled with the inadequate medical care he received and the poor newborn caring facilities available to him, meant that his life ended shortly after Begum's British citizenship was officially revoked. As a British citizen by birth, Jarrah was legally entitled to British aid and protection, yet he was not brought back to the UK when his health was most vulnerable despite requests from Begum's family to repatriate him. Begum's prophetic claim that she did not want to raise Jarrah in the detention camp because she feared he might die inside it became a focal point for the British public and mainstream news outlets. Questions were asked about the burden of responsibility for Jarrah's death, with many who supported Begum's right to return to the UK arguing that the sitting government failed in its responsibility to her child. Those who opposed Begum's right to return routinely placed the blame for Jarrah's death squarely with Begum.

This polarized view subsequently became a key topic of political debate that was later reckoned with in the House of Lords by Sajid Javid (then Home Secretary) and Diane Abbott (then Shadow Home Secretary). Apportioning the blame for Jarrah's death to Javid's decision not to repatriate him, Abbott argued that the British government failed in its duty to protect Jarrah and that both mother and baby should have been granted permission to return to the UK when it was initially requested. Refuting Javid's argument that it was impossible to extradite Jarrah from the camp because the UK does not have a consular presence in Syria, Abbott pointed to how numerous aid workers, doctors and journalists enter and leave the camp on a regular basis, making it highly possible for appointed UK officials to collect and transport Jarrah safely. Opposing viewpoints on who bears primary responsibility for Jarrah's death – Javid as the person who failed to repatriate him or Begum as the person who created the conditions that

---

[3]   Shamima was pregnant five times and had two miscarriages.

led to it – call attention to a broader ethics of blame, responsibility and duty that frame Begum's case. Had Begum's repatriation request been approved, Jarrah would likely have received the British health care that could have saved his life. Had Begum not left to join ISIS, Jarrah and her other two children would likely not have died from preventable illnesses that are very uncommon in Britain.

At the age of fifteen, under UK law Begum held criminal responsibility for her decision to join ISIS.[4] However, evidence shows that Begum was likely groomed and trafficked online by ISIS supporters who recognized and took advantage of her vulnerability. The details of Begum's activities whilst in ISIS are an unknown but prevalent topic of speculation. Begum is rumoured to have committed various acts of terrorism, including sewing ISIS members into suicide vests and strictly enforcing modesty laws through her purported role in Hisbah, ISIS's female 'morality police.' Begum has consistently denied these allegations, maintaining that she was nothing more than a mother and a housewife during the four years she spent with ISIS. For many, this role is enough to justify her loss of citizenship and her impending fate, but for others proof of her alleged acts of violence is necessary to determine her risk to other Britons if she were permitted to return.

At the time of writing, Begum resides in al-Roj detention camp in northern Syria with limited access to outside communication. She is under constant threat of violence from detainees who remain loyal to ISIS, and the current conditions of the camp and the makeshift facilities that she is indefinitely housed in means that Begum is at high risk of contracting illnesses linked to poor sanitation (i.e. cholera, diarrhoea or typhoid), temperature dysregulation (i.e. hypothermia) and infection (i.e. sepsis, Covid-19 and post-viral fatigue). Having already witnessed the slow suffering and death of her three young children, as well as the daily ravages of war and violence whilst living in former ISIS territory, it is reasonable to assume that Begum's mental health has considerably declined since she left Britain. Indeed, when reflecting on her initial response to losing her daughter with Joshua Baker, she notes that, had she not been pregnant with her second son at the time, she would have ended her life because of her grief. Existing within the confines of a loveless and abusive marriage and confronted with the daily threat of starvation and illness, she would have willingly followed her daughter who was, she argued, her reason for living.

Begum's international notoriety as an initially unrepentant 'ISIS bride,' along with her repeated failed attempts to regain British citizenship, has left her in prolonged legal limbo. As she remains indefinitely detained in what has often been described as an 'open-air prison,' her mental health is likely to deteriorate further. In this chapter, I draw on media coverage of Begum's case and public responses to interviews Begum gave to evaluate the perceived relationship between culpability, deservedness and grievability when it comes to health and the right to life for people guilty of terrorist offences. This chapter will further consider the humanitarian and political implications of Begum's (un)grievability by critically analysing her guilt

---

[4] The age of criminal responsibility in England, Wales and Northern Ireland is ten years old.

in joining ISIS in relation to her current position of statelessness and indefinite detention. I argue that the media-fuelled notoriety surrounding Begum helped shape a political climate that enabled the UK Home Office to justify stripping her of British citizenship – a decision that has serious implications for her health and well-being, both now and in the future.

Guilty and (un)grievable

Shamima Begum knowingly joined a terrorist organization following months of online grooming and exposure to online ISIS propaganda depicting the newly established 'caliphate' as an Islamic utopia. When reflecting on her initial recognition of ISIS as a utopic homeland, Begum routinely described the iconic funfair often shown in ISIS propaganda videos and the fantasy of what life could be for Muslims seeking to establish their faith as a foundational tenant of their everyday being. In doing so, Begum arguably demonstrates a conceivable 'innocence' rooted in a naïve belief in the possibility of joy and a miscalculation of the consequences that awaited her.

The hope that Begum had of living a happy life under ISIS, while not realized, played a fundamental role in her decision to leave Britain. This hope, recounted retrospectively, encapsulates both the naïve starting point from which Begum formed her decision and the disillusioned endpoint from which that decision was realized. Speaking as an indefinite detainee in al-Roj detention camp, Begum's characterization of her initial impression of ISIS as utopic is consistent with media arts scholar Jayna Brown's description of utopia as a term that is often pejoratively used 'to indicate the failure of a humanistic project … or to acclaim the hope of its fulfilment, the achievement of the good life, in which all our earthly needs would be met by a given system' (Brown 2021: 4). Begum's defection was driven by an illusory vision of Islamic euphoria promised by ISIS. For Begum and others drawn by similar beliefs, this dream was a failure from the outset.

Begum's purported expectation once she joined ISIS was that she would marry, have children, and 'live a pure Islamic life' that allowed her to practice and fully explore her developing faith in Islam. When pressed about how she felt when leaving Britain knowing that she would likely never see it again Begum told one interviewer that she felt somewhat relieved. This relief, we later discover, derived from Begum's feelings of displacement and foreignness in Britain as both a Muslim girl and a person of Bengali descent. Feeling neither British nor Bengali, Begum found it difficult to reconcile who she was with the country she was raised in throughout much of her young life. This, Begum argues, made her particularly susceptible to ISIS grooming tactics and vulnerable to a society that promised to accept and support all Muslims regardless of their country of origin.

Unlike the other case studies featured in this book, Begum's offers nuance when considering the relationship between grievability, individual fault and state-sanctioned racism by clearly aligning (un)grievability with public responses to proven crime. Begum's guilt in joining ISIS is, for many, unequivocal, however equivocal her actual role in ISIS might be.[5] Her initial lack of repentance and subsequent denial of any responsibility for the violent crimes perpetrated by ISIS that, she argues, were separate from her domestic role – namely public executions of foreign 'enemies' and the torture of those who oppose or fail to comply with ISIS codes of conduct – fanned the flames of public outrage following Begum's initial discovery. Her response to details of acts of terror committed by ISIS abroad, most notably the 2017 UK Manchester Arena attack that saw twenty-two civilians die after an ISIS fighter detonated a home-made bomb in a contained venue, was particularly noted by Britons who subsequently understood Begum's lack of remorse as evidence of her continued threat to the UK and, later, as justification for her citizenship denial and ensuing exile. In her book *The Monstrous & the Vulnerable: Framing British Jihadi Brides* Leonie Jackson attributes this response to Begum's lack of empathy with ISIS victims and her lack of contrition for her role in supporting ISIS attacks, even if indirectly. 'As an ideal victim,' Jackson writes, '[Begum] was expected to behave in a particular way: to renounce ISIS, to be contrite, to speak of her shame in joining the group, and to ask for forgiveness. When Begum did not play the role assigned to the passive victim, her evaluation as vulnerable was untenable' (Jackson 2022: 192).

The binary Jackson presents – villain or victim – fails to account for the confluence of Begum's guilt in joining ISIS and her naivety in doing so at the age of fifteen following months of purported grooming and online coercion. As arguably *both* a villain and a victim, Begum's inhabits a positionality that renders her (un)grievability subject to the viewpoint of the accuser who, depending on their political orientation, might see her as either a villain or a victim or both. At the time of writing, public support for Begum's citizenship deprivation routinely hinges on these political orientations, rendering them instrumental in recognizing Begum's fate as a matter of public interest. Each time an appeal to re-instate Begum's British citizenship is made – often based on the claim that she was trafficked and groomed as a minor – it reaches news headlines and re-emerges as a key topic of political debate not because new information is made available but because the question of her (un)grievability remains unsolved. How can we reckon Begum's proven criminal act(s) in joining ISIS with the fact that she was likely groomed and trafficked as a child which, some argue, diminishes her responsibility for any wrongdoing?

At fifteen years old, Begum was, under UK law, a child who was repeatedly raped by her then husband and subsequently entangled in a domestic life from which she was unable to leave as a 'woman' under ISIS control. How, then, can we reconcile the argument that Begum should have left ISIS immediately after she saw that it was not a utopic homeland for Muslims with the practical reality that she was unable to do so given the lethal consequences of ISIS desertion? And what does it mean for the then Home Secretary, on behalf of the UK government and with the support of British people who ratified his decision to revoke Begum's citizenship, to endanger Begum's life knowingly and significantly by permanently exiling her from Britain?

---

[5]	Begum is purported to have committed a number of offences whilst a member of IS, including sewing suicide vests and being a member of 'hesbah'.

The biopolitical project of 'making live and letting die' offers an appropriate, although limited, framework through which to understand these questions. Begum's (arguably diminished) responsibility in committing acts of terror, and the continued threat she allegedly poses to other Britons because of those past acts and classified intelligence information indicating that she might commit similar acts in future, offer the primary justifications for her citizenship removal. If Begum were to be permitted re-entry into Britain, this argument follows, she would likely endanger the lives of ordinary 'innocent' citizens by conspiring to commit future acts of terrorism. In this way and following this logic, to 'make [the broader population] live' one must 'let [the threat] die', a political act that counters democratic recognitions of individual value with a utilitarian ethos of the need to preserve the many over the few. This prioritization of some lives over others, rooted in beliefs about fairness and predicated on binary perceptions of innocence and guilt, presents and upholds grievability as a political motivation by assigning grievability to the 'innocent' many and denying it to the 'guilty' few. Recognizing Begum as guilty, then, becomes a necessary tool in constructing her as ungrievable because of the moral socio-political conflation between grievability and innocence. Following this logic, the biopolitical project of leaving Begum to 'rot' in al-Roj detention camp becomes a justified and appropriate response to Begum's individual actions, actions which later placed her outside the boundaries of care and compassion and, for some, beyond the boundaries of forgiveness.

For those who do extend care, compassion and forgiveness to Begum, her citizenship deprivation and indefinite exile are routinely understood as decisions that extend beyond the biopolitical aim of 'making [some] live' and 'letting [her] die' because they constitute what Achille Mbembe describes as a necropolitical aim of 'letting [some] live' and 'making [her] die.' In his book *Necropolitics*, Mbembe describes what he sees as the failure of biopower to adequately encapsulate life courses that are shaped, and in many cases determined, by external recognitions of (non) human value that are assigned and implemented by ruling systems of power. Mbembe argues,

> the notion of biopower is insufficient to account for the various ways in which, in our contemporary world, weapons are deployed in the interest of maximally destroying persons and creating death-worlds, that is, new and unique forms of social existence in which vast populations are subjected to living conditions that confer upon them the status of the living dead.
>
> (Mbembe 2019: 92)

The production of 'death-worlds' as realms in which the 'living dead' reside offers a useful metaphor to understand the positionality of all persons considered ungrievable in terms of their relation to the state. The 'living dead's' abjection, derived from their recognition as 'non-human,' casts them into a world where they are, effectively, dead despite being alive. As the 'living dead' they are refigured as ghosts who haunt the 'living' in ways that reaffirm what it means to live.

By recognizing the 'living dead' as existing outside the boundaries of the human, we can understand what it means to be human and to subsequently enjoy all the privileges and delights that position affords us. Taking freedom for granted, it is easy for most people in the UK to overlook and/or undermine what it means to be imprisoned and exiled in a foreign country. Moreover, when coupled with the presumption of guilt that seemingly justifies reasons for imprisonment, it is easy to purposefully avoid extending sympathy to people who seemingly abused the privileges and delights of freedom when they had it. Accused of turning her back on British values and the democracy that upholds them, Begum – under this logic – is disqualified from human life by those who relegate her to her current home – the 'death-world' that is the al-Roj camp. As the 'living dead' Begum is expected to rot within this 'death-world' as both a punishment for her crime and a consequence of her actions. Following her many failed legal appeals, this is a fate that Begum has seemingly accepted. In an interview with Baker in 2023, Begum was asked if she believed she would return to Britain in the foreseeable future, to which she replied with a swift 'nope.' This 'nope' was shortly followed by her rationale that 'ISIS was the worst thing of the twenty-first century and I was a part of it and now I have to face the consequences of my actions, and this camp is the consequence of my actions' (BBC 2023). The practical implications of this consequence, and its health effects, are severe.

Health precarity in Syrian ISIS detention camps: a looming crisis

There are two detention camps that house the former ISIS families who, prior to their detention, lived in ISIS-controlled Syrian territories. Most of these detainees are women and around 60 per cent of them are children, many of whom were born in the camps and know little of life outside of them. Both camps – al-Hol and al-Roj – are located in northeastern Syria and, at the time of writing, remain under the armed control of the Syrian Democratic Forces (SDF) who fought against ISIS during their occupation of key Syrian sites and cities (most notably Raqqa). The camps are split into sections, housing different groups of people largely in accordance with their nationality. One section of the larger and more notorious of the two camps, al-Hol, is locally referred to as 'the caliphate' because of the overwhelming number of people who remain loyal to ISIS within its barbed-wire walls (Sky News 2024). This section, also known as the Annex, is home to roughly forty-thousand foreign nationals who defected from countries including China, Trinidad, Sweden, Russia, the USA and the UK to join ISIS during its stronghold. Unlike many of the Syrian and Iraqi detainees who were absorbed into ISIS territory and later imprisoned in this camp, those hailing from foreign countries are believed to be acutely dangerous because they chose – and planned – to join ISIS. As noted by Anand Gopal in their reporting of the camp's conditions and how people came to be there, '[m]any of the women [in the Annex], unlike those in the rest of the camp, chose to join the Islamic State; they are among the most extreme of the true believers' (Gopal 2024).

In both camps, makeshift tents (most of which are donated from charities and international aid organizations) are firmly pegged into sand and tightly packed together in concentrated rows that, from a distance, appear to form communities. Vast stretches of these grey and cream-coloured tents are punctuated by brightly coloured clothing that hangs loosely from washing lines. These clothing items chiefly belong to the children; most of the women continue to dress in full niqab as they did when living in ISIS territory. The conditions of the camps are desperate and squalid, with extreme weather and poor sanitation facilitating the rampant spread of disease. Food is rationed and often scarce, mostly distributed by either SDF officers or foreign aid workers. The overwhelming presence of children playing in, around or on sewage ditches, wells, mud and endless stretches of sand is constant.

Between the streets of tents are makeshift markets selling fruits, vegetables, clothing, ice cream, hair dye and other everyday items. Some detainees work in these markets to gain an income, which many then use to supplement the food rations they are allocated. According to one al-Hol resident interviewed by a journalist in 2022, residents receive one monthly food basket from aid organizations. This basket does not contain eggs, milk, fruit, vegetables or meat, which means that all must be supplemented by items found in the markets. At the time this person was interviewed, one carton of fourteen eggs reportedly cost around fourteen thousand Syrian lira (roughly $5 USD) which, this person noted, meant that most families without a supplemental income could not afford them (Khubieh 2022). The limited availability of fresh and nutritious food for the poorer residents of al-Hol has clear negative implications for their health, making them more susceptible to nutrition-related diseases and decreasing their capacity to recover swiftly from infection and serious illness.

For the camp's growing children who make up the bulk of its population, this limited availability of food has particularly dire implications for their physical, mental and emotional development. According to a report conducted by *Save the Children* in 2020, during that year and within a period of five days, five children in al-Hol camp died from preventable causes, including severe malnutrition. The circumstances that brought about their deaths were further exacerbated by the Covid-19 pandemic, which reduced the capacity of local health services to treat children in need by 40 per cent due to restrictions on travel in and out of the camps (Save The Children 2021). In 2019, UNICEF launched a malnutrition screening campaign for children in al-Hol who had, at that point, begun to arrive at the camp in waves, often following days of travel by foot fleeing war in former ISIS territory. UNICEF's initial aim to administer preventative aid and treatment to 24,000 children in al-Hol under the age of five is telling of the scale of the crisis (UNICEF, 2019).

In both al-Hol and al-Roj camps, lack of clean water is routinely cited as a critical health concern. Adults surveyed by *Save the Children* in 2021 noted that the 'quality and quantity of the water and food in the camp is very poor, and the available WASH [Water, Sanitation and Hygiene] infrastructure is inadequate' for the number of people who are reliant on it (Save The Children 2021). According to one rapid assessment in March 2019, when the al-Hol population was at its peak, 2,545 latrines were available to accommodate 70,480 residents (roughly twenty-eight residents per latrine). Many of these latrines were in disrepair and, in some phases of the camp, up to 68 per cent were unusable (WASH 2019). Because residents commonly experience sanitation issues with communal latrines that are overpopulated, lack lighting and do not have adequate water for sanitation (RAND 2023), some have dug private holes around their tents that serve as alternative latrines. This consequently increases the prevalence of disease and illness associated with the camp's defunct sewage system.

Medical facilities in both camps are scarce. In al-Hol, limited medical and dental services are available in the Main Camp at cost to the residents (Save The Children 2021), rendering those who are unable to pay particularly vulnerable to serious illness and premature death from illnesses that arise because of the camp's conditions. According to *Save the Children*, in al-Roj there is one medical unit with basic services to cater to the needs of its population of 2,600 (Save The Children 2021). If detainees require urgent treatment that is not provided by the camp's medical facilities they are referred to local hospitals, where they are permitted to go if they obtain the correct authorization. Obtaining this authorization is often challenging and time-consuming, which can significantly delay the treatment needed by detainees with life-threatening conditions. Across both camps, most child deaths occur because of acute malnutrition, diarrhoea and fire-related injuries. Acute malnutrition and diarrhoea largely occur because of poor infrastructures that limit access to nutritious and plentiful diets, clean water and adequate sanitation. Fire-related injuries are driven by two primary causes – accidental fire from electric heaters and cookers that are kept within tents and deliberate arson. Inside the residents' tents makeshift beds, rugs, heaters, cookers, utensils and children's toys often coalesce in the small space afforded to each family. Children interviewed by *Save the Children* in 2020 cited accidental fires as one of their key everyday concerns, particularly in winter when heaters are frequently relied on for warmth. In al-Roj in 2020, three children died and two were critically injured in two separate incidents after their heaters set fire to their tents (Save The Children 2021).

In both camps, the threat of arson from ISIS loyalists remains constant. Those who speak out against ISIS (and their children) are at high risk of attack from residents who remain loyal to ISIS and pray for its resurgence. Indeed, during one interview, when challenged about her initial justification of ISIS's terrorist acts as forms of retaliation against the West, Shamima Begum cited her fear of 'the women' as her primary motive. These 'women,' she claimed, are residents in the camp who are known to have set fire to the tents of people who have publicly defied ISIS whilst they, and their children, were sleeping. Having recently given birth and feeling protective over her newborn son, Begum claimed she would have feared for his life (as well as her own) if she had chosen to publicly disclose her negative feelings towards ISIS.

At the time of writing, the media notoriety Begum gained following her discovery in al-Hol in 2019, and her subsequent denouncement of ISIS, means that she is at constant risk of harm from the many ISIS loyalists who remain inside the camps. Shortly after her first interview, Begum was moved to al-Roj as a security precaution. This camp, while comparably safer, remains unsafe for women like Begum who publicly oppose ISIS ideology. When asked about life inside al-Roj camp by journalist and film-maker Andrew Drury in 2022, Begum and another detainee, Hoda, reacted cautiously. Sitting next to the dusty remains of a former tent that had been burned down in a deliberate arson attack, Hoda describes their situation as 'scary,' arguing that 'in the camp you can also not talk too freely because when they [journalists] put something online the whole camp can [see it]. Phones are forbidden here but people have a phone and they look for it [videos of what people say]. They will find it and in the end we are the ones who are in danger' (GB News 2022).

Living under conditions that generate constant fear of imminent danger has severe implications for both mental and physical health. The stress that comes from not knowing when and where an attack will happen, whether that attack will cause serious injury, whether it will be fatal, or if loved ones will also be harmed by it can have devastating effects on those who live in 'open-air prisons.' These prisons can be more effectively understood as cages that permit detainees a semblance of freedom by allowing them to walk freely within their confines whilst simultaneously ensuring they cannot reach beyond them. The self-governed nature of these prisons, guarded by armed officials who secure their perimeters and exist largely on their periphery, means that the impending threat of violence is often unmanageable, unpredictable and, for many inmates, inevitable.

Indefinite detention, a prospect that sees detainees imprisoned for unspecified periods of time (most often before they have been legally tried), is routinely described by civil and humanitarian rights organizations as a violation of basic human rights. The chronic hopelessness that often accompanies failed legal appeals, recurrent interactions with unsympathetic prison guards, daily threats of violence and the daily indignities of living in the squalid conditions of the camps renders detainees at high risk of multiple health conditions including depression, anxiety and suicidal ideation. In *Precarious Life: The Powers of Mourning and Violence*, Judith Butler urges readers to consider the biopolitical implications of indefinite detention when implemented by the state and on the premise that the prisoner's indefinite detention is in the interests of national security. Using the indefinite detention of prisoners in US-controlled Guantánamo Bay as an example, Butler notes the intrinsic dehumanization rooted in this practice. They write,

> It is crucial to ask under what conditions some human lives cease to become eligible for basic, if not universal, human rights. How does the US government construe these conditions? And to what extent is there a racial and ethnic frame through which these imprisoned lives are viewed and judged so that they are deemed less human, or as having departed from the recognisable human community?
>
> (Butler 2020: 45)

By questioning the construal of conditions that prevent some lives from being fully recognized as lives, Butler shows how 'humanness' is understood in relation to rights that are deemed inalienable – namely, the right to a fair trial and to clearly demarcated prison time when found guilty of a punishable crime. Additionally, by questioning whether racial and ethnic differences frame imprisoned lives in relation to their 'humanness' and associated treatment, Butler interrogates the inner workings of racism in political decisions about indefinite detention. In doing so Butler raises important questions about how crime and punishment are conceived in relation to the accused or guilty, notably: who is left to languish in despair not knowing how long they will have to endure their unendurable living conditions? Who is spared this cruelty through expedited legal action? To what extent do racist logics that constitute the human/non-human inform these decisions? And how do these decisions, in turn, reify the boundaries of the human/non-human?

In the case of Shamima Begum, her guilt in joining ISIS, coupled with unverified rumours of her involvement in various acts of terror during the four years she spent living in ISIS territory, are routinely cited as justifications for her citizenship deprivation and exile. As such, Begum's indefinite detention is habitually cited as an outcome of her own poor decision-making and foolish choices rather than a situation brought about by the state. The health risks Begum faces during her indefinite detention in al-Roj are, in this way, rationalized as deserved outcomes of a decision that she made and had full control over. This argument exists despite evidence that she was likely trafficked and groomed online prior to her defection. In this way, Begum's guilt places her outside the boundaries of the human and, thus, beyond the political imperative to implement care and extend humanitarian sympathy and/or aid. Expulsion from humanity, Hannah Arendt notes, naturally follows from citizenship loss because the subject is made vulnerable to arbitrary political decisions through their subsequent precarity. According to Arendt, human rights are inextricably anchored to the state because the state affords inalienable protections to its citizens (Arendt 2017). Without citizenship, stateless former citizens are vulnerable to harm because they do not have access to vital protections. Decisions to deprive citizens of their citizenship necessitate assurances that are intended to protect the person in question from the inevitable harms that accompany statelessness.

Understanding what it means to be Brit(ish): establishing grievability through citizenship

When the then UK Home Secretary, Sajid Javid, stripped Begum of her British citizenship in 2019 he did so under the pretext that this decision would not render her stateless. Because Begum had an alternative claim to Bangladeshi citizenship she was entitled to Bangladeshi citizenship if she claimed it. Begum has never visited Bangladesh and knows little of its customs or traditions. Shortly after she was informed of this alternative, Begum was made aware of the likelihood that she would be arrested and hanged for her involvement in ISIS if she were to arrive in Bangladesh to claim her citizenship. As the wife of a Dutch national, Begum later expressed her hope that she could claim citizenship in the Netherlands. At the time of writing, this option remains unavailable to her.

Under section 40 of the British Nationality Act 1981, and in accordance with the Nationality and Borders Bill, UK citizenship deprivation is 'used against those who obtained citizenship by fraud and against the most dangerous people, such as terrorists, extremist and serious organised criminals' (UK Home Office 2023). When citizenship deprivation is recognized by the UK Home Office as 'conducive to the public good,' the Nationality and Borders Bill allows the Home Office to deprive a person of their citizenship without prior notification in exceptional circumstances (UK Home Office

2023). Each case is individually decided by the Home Secretary (UK Home Office 2023). The precarity of Begum's political situation, as a stateless indefinite detainee in a detention camp in northern Syria, is made possible because of a legal loophole that facilitates a technical reading of Begum's legal position rather than a practical or, indeed many would argue, moral reading of it.

While Javid's decision was *technically* legal because it would not render Begum stateless if she acted on her right to Bangladeshi citizenship, it was *practically void* because it offered an alternative that amounted to a death sentence. In the UK, where capital punishment is illegal, many (including Begum) puzzled over the use of Bangladeshi citizenship as a legal justification for Begum's citizenship deprivation given the lethal consequences of enacting this claim. How, many wondered, could this justification be used by the UK Home Secretary when it effectively invoked a death sentence? How could the UK maintain its opposition to capital punishment whilst indirectly permitting it? And what does this mean for other British nationals who also have a claim to alternative citizenship(s) through parental and/or familial ties and go on to commit crimes abroad?

When asked this question by a British person of Indian descent, right-wing British journalist Nana Akua responded by saying 'don't commit the crime' (GB News 2023). This dismissive invocation – shared by many on social media – not only fails to answer the question but also points to a demarcation of citizenship in accordance with perceptions of deservedness. Rather than recognizing citizenship as an entitlement that people have based on where they were born, raised and/or grew up, Akua and like-minded others support citizenship precarity when it is implemented in response to criminal activity. Citizenship, when conceptualized this way, is inculcated in a politics of responsibility that affords citizenship to some and not others depending on their individual conduct. For those who hold this view, citizenship is envisaged as an *earned attribute* rather than a *legal entitlement*.

In majority White countries like the UK, laws that permit citizenship deprivation for British nationals if they hold alternative citizenship(s), or alternative claims to citizenship(s), disproportionately disadvantage Black and Brown people who are, on average, more likely to have at least one parent from an immigrant background than their White peers. In this way, citizenship precarity can be understood as a racialized disadvantage that disproportionately impacts people of colour. In February 2024, Conservative politician Jacob Rees-Mogg surprised many by arguing that Begum's citizen deprivation unfairly suggests a two-tier system for British nationals along racial lines. Writing in the conservative political magazine *The Spectator* he states,

> The ability to deprive people, who have a claim to another citizenship, of their British passport, creates two categories of Briton. Those with no right to another nationality are in the first-class carriage. Whatever they do, they cannot be made an exile or outlaw and expelled from the country. On the other hand, those who themselves came to the UK or whose parents did so are in the second-class carriage. They may be stripped of their citizenship even if they have never claimed another foreign nationality or even visited the country. This is a fundamentally

racist policy as it denies the absolute Britishness of all those who are either recent immigrants themselves or their children.

(Rees-Mogg 2023)

Rees-Mogg's use of the term 'absolute Britishness' is interesting to note here. While seemingly liberal in how it is applied to all people who have, or successfully gain, British citizenship (including recent migrants and their descendants), Britishness is routinely contested by those who recognize it as a cultural identity that excludes certain groups (namely those who are not 'native born' and/or White). Indeed, when asked about her motivation to join ISIS, Begum partially attributed this decision to her feeling of not being British or Bengali but both and, consequently, neither. Because these two identities are incompatible in a context that remains Islamophobic and, thus, largely unaccepting of cultural and religious differences, it is difficult for Britons like Begum to claim Britishness whilst also having seemingly opposing identity markers. This difficulty is often lost in discussions that adopt post-racialism at point of entry and, consequently, overlook nuanced claims of Britishness that do (or do not) align with how Britishness is broadly socially and culturally conceived.

In 2022, Begum began appearing in interviews with mainstream news outlets wearing 'Western' clothes. These outfits – including tank tops, yoga pants and baseball caps – marked a notable departure from her usual Islamic dress and raised eyebrows from sceptics who accused her of trying to 'look British' to garner support. For many, it demonstrated a superficial attempt to perform British assimilation and cast off her former ties to ISIS.[6] These sartorial changes raise important questions about how visual and cultural cues are understood to influence the perception of a person's grievability. Is her choice to adopt 'Western' clothing a genuine reflection of personal change, or merely a strategic performance aimed at a British audience? Why does Begum feel the need to 'look British' to be considered British? And what does this tell us about the conditions under which empathy and inclusion are extended – or withheld? Begum's attempts to visually distance herself from her past compel us to interrogate who is deemed grievable, and whether grievability is, in fact, contingent on embodying certain cultural or nationalistic traits.

References

Arendt, H. (2017), *On the Origins of Totalitarianism*. Penguin.

Baker, J. (2022), 'Shamima Begum: Spy for Canada Smuggled Schoolgirl to Syria', *BBC News*, https://www.bbc.co.uk/news/uk-62726954 (accessed 23 September 2024).

BBC. (2023), 'The Shamima Begum Story', https://www.bbc.co.uk/iplayer/episode/m001j079/the-shamima-begum-story (accessed 24 September 2024).

Brown, J. (2021), *Black Utopias: Speculative Life and the Music of Other Worlds*. Duke University Press.

---

[6] When questioned, Shamima made clear that this shift was for her and not for others.

Butler, J. (2020), *Precarious Life: The Powers of Mourning and Violence*. Verso.

Dodd, V. and A. Gani. (2015), 'Police Failed Us, Say Families of Girls Feared to Have Gone to Syria', *The Guardian*, https://www.theguardian.com/uk-news/2015/mar/06/syria-bound-girls-hid-police-letter-families (accessed 22 September 2024).

GB News. (2022), 'Watch Our Exclusive Interview with Shamima Begum in Full', https://www.youtube.com/watch?v=jJ8bsQFzLL0 (accessed 21 September 2024).

GB News. (2023), 'Is Shamima Begum the UK's Responsibility?', https://www.youtube.com/watch?v=n8Y4Qs29kiE (accessed 2 September 2024).

Gopal, A. (2024), 'The Open-Air Prisons for ISIS Supporters – and Victims', https://www.newyorker.com/magazine/2024/03/18/the-open-air-prison-for-isis-supporters-and-victims (accessed 30 April 2024).

Jackson, L. (2022), *The Monstrous & the Vulnerable: Framing British Jihadi Brides*. Oxford University Press.

Khubieh, S. (2022), 'Abandoned to their Fate: Children Die from Hunger and Disease in Syria's Al-Hol Camp as World Turns its Back', *The New Arab*, https://www.newarab.com/features/al-hol-camp-dire-conditions-are-deathtrap-children (accessed 3 September 2024).

Mbembe, A. (2019), *Necropolitics*. Duke University Press.

RAND. (2023), 'In the Wreckage of ISIS: An Examination of Challenges Confronting Detained and Displaced Populations in Northeastern Syria', https://www.rand.org/content/dam/rand/pubs/research_reports/RRA400/RRA471-1/RAND_RRA471-1.pdf (accessed 12 September 2024).

Rees-Mogg, J. (2023), 'Shamima Begum Shouldn't Have Lost her British Citizenship', *The Spectator*, https://www.spectator.co.uk/article/shamima-begum-shouldnt-have-lost-her-british-citizenship (accessed 24 September 2024).

Save The Children. (2021), 'When am I Going to Start to Live?', https://resourcecentre.savethechildren.net/document/when-am-i-going-start-live-urgent-need-repatriate-foreign-children-trapped-al-hol-and-roj (accessed 25 September 2024).

Sky News. (2019), 'Shamima Begum: I didn't do anything dangerous', https://www.youtube.com/watch?v=EWcJHxmXD1Q (accessed 20 September 2024).

Sky News. (2024), 'Syria: Inside Al Hol Refugee Camp Where Shamima Begum was Held', https://www.youtube.com/watch?v=1i8G403cblA (accessed 24 September 2024).

The Times. (2019), 'Exclusive interview with Shamima Begum, Bethnal Green girl who fled to Syria', https://www.youtube.com/watch?v=SooDVtENq9c (accessed 21 September 2024).

UK Home Office. (2023), 'Nationality and Borders Bill: Deprivation of Citizenship Factsheet', https://www.gov.uk/government/publications/nationality-and-borders-bill-deprivation-of-citizenship-factsheet/nationality-and-borders-bill-deprivation-of-citizenship-factsheet#process-and-safeguards-already-in-place (accessed 3 September 2024).

UNICEF. (2019), 'UNICEF treats children in Al-Hol camp, Syria for malnutrition', https://www.unicef.org/syria/stories/unicef-treats-children-al-hol-camp-syria-malnutrition, (accessed 21 September 2024).

WASH. (2019), 'Northeast Syria – Al Hol Refugee/ IDP Camp, Water, Sanitation, and Hygiene (WASH) Rapid Assessment: 14-19 March, 2019', https://reliefweb.int/report/syrian-arab-republic/northeast-syria-al-hol-refugeeidp-camp-water-sanitation-and-hygiene-wash (accessed 29 September 2024).

5

Child Death, Visual Consumption and Grievability Politics: Remembering Alan Kurdi

In their discussion of war and suffering, and specifically war and suffering that is viewed by warring parties as a legitimate way to achieve peace and justice, Judith Butler points to the numerous children killed by Israeli soldiers in their pursuit of Hamas to question the material realities of war in the context of grievability. Highlighting their reduced personhood and subsequent status as material objects in war, Butler shows how Palestinian children's capacity as grievable subjects is denied through their framing as 'collateral damage', which is conceived of as an unfortunate (though likely) outcome of war by Israeli politicians and media outlets. They write,

> There are those in the Israeli press who say that if civilians were killed, if children were killed, it was because Hamas hides itself in civilian centers, uses children to shield itself, and so sets up the situation in which Israel must kill civilians and children in order to defend itself, legitimately, against Hamas. Hamas is accused of 'cynically' using children and civilian centers to hide its own armaments. There are several sources that can document the untruth of these claims, but for the moment, let us consider how this argument works. If the Palestinian children who are killed by mortar and phosphorous bombs are human shields, then they are not children at all, but rather bits of armament, military instruments and materiel, aiding and abetting an assault on Israel.
>
> (Butler, 2016: xxvi)

In making this provocation, Butler offers two key suggestions. Firstly, that attributing responsibility for innocent deaths to the opposing side confers a strategic aim of 'legitimizing' those deaths as a necessary outcome of war. If opposition forces had not carried out the initial threat of violence, this reasoning suggests, these children would not have died through retaliatory action. In other words, because Israel can frame those deaths as an outcome of self-defence, they are able to publicly absolve themselves of responsibility for them. Secondly, portraying the deaths of Palestinian children as a tragic but necessary consequence of Israeli 'self-defence' renders these children non-human, inconsequential and ultimately ungrievable. By framing them as 'bits of armament, military instruments and material', the Israeli press denies these children's humanity by negating their fleshy materiality. These children are not seen as children but as material objects and they are consequently refused the protections civilians are ostensibly afforded when exposed to military violence through war and conflict.

Children are violently afflicted by war in multiple ways. As Butler notes, some get caught up in the crossfire of opposing regimes, rendering their death collateral damage in an ongoing pursuit of 'national security.' As we saw in the previous chapter, some children are forced to exist indefinitely in makeshift displacement camps that directly compromise their mental and physical health. Others experience trauma fleeing war zones through perilous escape routes and border crossings. These experiences illustrate the ripple effects of war, whereby mobility and immobility are structurally determined by local violence and political instability. At the time of writing, ongoing armed conflicts in multiple parts of the world, and the consequent rise in border crossings into Europe by people fleeing those conflicts, have generated political polarization in Britain between those who fear a 'foreign invasion' and those who recognize a moral imperative to grant asylum to people involuntarily displaced by war.

In September 2015, photographs of the lifeless body of three-year-old Alan Kurdi, washed ashore in Bodrum, Turkey, circulated widely on social and mainstream media, shocking viewers around the world. Of the two principal images that were circulated – one depicting Alan being gently lifted by a Turkish police officer, and the other showing him lying face-down and alone – the latter is particularly poignant. Describing this image presents a challenge: its emotional impact resists easy articulation, and any attempt to capture it risks oversimplification. I will, however, attempt it. Alan's tiny body, dressed in blue shorts and a red t-shirt, lies at the meeting point between the sea and the beach. His face is partially turned away from the camera, his right cheek submerged in sand, his eyes closed. His arms lay at the side of his body with his palms turned upward. Alan looks as though he may be sleeping, which intensifies the harrowing sensation that accompanies viewing the image knowing that he is dead. As a viewer, the pathos generated by this image is intricately tied to the impulse I feel to pick him up and gently wake him up. Knowing this cannot be done means that I am stuck in an affective limbo, unable to move on from the image because of its uncanny resemblance to images of sleeping children who will almost certainly wake up.

I do not include my own affective responses to this image here to suggest they are naturally, or indeed universally, felt. As I note later in this chapter, others have responded to this image in ways that directly juxtapose my emotive engagement with it. Rather, I include them as a starting point to think through the productive capacity of images like this one that convey the horrors of war through child death and suffering. In doing so, I seek to highlight the role of innocence in affective registers that confer grievability because they recognize injustice and external culpability. For the countless children who die every day because of war-induced precarity and displacement this conference is often bestowed posthumously, rendering it meaningless to the lives that are lost because they are not seen as grievable whilst alive.

Returning to Butler's contention that Palestinian children are reduced to 'military instruments' in Israel's pursuit of Hamas, what does it mean to recognize children as collateral damage in wars that are waged to protect vulnerable nation states? Which children in these wars are protected and preserved? How is their innocence framed within the context of their grievability? And what does it mean to permit or overlook their death when it is seen as a necessary outcome of efforts towards national security? In this chapter, I discuss the efficacy of undisputed innocence in social justice efforts that seek to preserve life and promote health amongst children fleeing or living in war zones, calling attention to the power and limits of digital media in generating recognitions of grievability for refugees and internally displaced groups. By focusing on circulated images of children as innocent victims of war and displacement that are mobilized to garner international support, I question the uses of collectively recognizing a child's grievability when that recognition fails to translate into political action. Or, in the words of Susie Linfield, I ask '[w]hat does it mean to acknowledge another's suffering, knowing full well that to embrace it is impossible?' (Linfield 2010: xvi). By placing public responses to Alan's death in conversation with similar responses to visual depictions of other children who are displaced victims of war, I further examine the moral and ethical implications of acknowledging the grievability of child refugees while failing to act on that recognition to promote change.

Affective engagement through visual consumption

Photography is often used in service of social justice efforts to expose, condemn and radically alter contemporary manifestations of systemic violence. The advent of video capture, particularly through smartphone technology, has generated interest in the political potential of recording and circulating violent digital content in real time to global audiences as a form of protest. In his 2018 music video for his song *This is America*, Donald Glover (also known by his stage name Childish Gambino) offers a commentary on the radical potential of capturing clear instances of anti-Black violence through cell phone technology whilst simultaneously evoking its futility in ultimately stopping this violence. Throughout this video, Glover satirizes the senseless killing of Black people while they are acting in ways that are both ordinary and – in the USA – largely respected. The first killing is of a Black man playing a guitar, who is approached by Glover from behind and shot in the back of his head. The second is of a church choir, who are impulsively shot with a semi-automatic rifle while worshipping – a scene reminiscent of the 2015 murder of nine Black church worshippers in Charleston, South Carolina by self-professed White supremacist Dylann Roof.[1] Dancing with a group of school-uniform clad teenagers amidst a backdrop of anti-police riots, Glover maintains a wide smile while staring directly at the camera and repeating the refrain 'this is America.' Despite noting the importance of the onlookers' cell phones in capturing the injustices taking place in real time, Glover denotes the continuation of senseless violence to underscore its entrenchment within US culture. The linear nature

---

[1] In June 2015, Dylann Roof murdered nine people in a church shooting in Charleston, South Carolina. At the time of writing, he is on death row in Terre Haute Federal Prison in Indiana.

of systemic racism evoked throughout this video speaks to the need to recognize racism as an ongoing problem despite brief moments of reprieve.

When individual images produce affective responses from viewers who have the capacity to effect change, whether through direct policy responses or democratic participation, it is important that these responses are translated into meaningful political action. When they are not translated, Glover suggests, the senseless violence persists and Black people remain in precarious environments where survival is perilous. By speaking to the long-term futility of images that depict anti-Black violence without spurring radical change, Glover encourages viewers to move beyond the image to see the bigger picture – one that requires a radical redress of histories of anti-Black violence.

In her book *Listening to Images*, Tina Campt notes the importance of moving beyond a superficial reading of images to realize their affective potentials. In a similar way to how Glover requires his viewers to see past his wide smile and jubilant dancing to the violence taking place behind him, Campt encourages readers to look beyond the surface-level value of images to unearth their 'sound.' She writes,

> [L]istening to images is constituted as a practice of looking beyond what we see and attuning our sense to the other affective frequencies through which photographs register. It is a haptic encounter that foregrounds the frequencies of images and how they move, touch, and connect us to the event of the photo. Such a connection may begin as a practice of 'careful looking,' but it does not end there.
>
> (Campt 2017: 9)

The 'event' of the photo that Campt refers to is located in its broader socio-political context, which encompasses those who are not captured in the photograph's frame. In other words, the broader significance of individual depictions of violence speaks to the circumstances of countless others with similar experiences. Listening to Alan Kurdi's image, lifeless and washed up on a foreign beach after a perilous journey across the Mediterranean Sea, requires attending to its resonance as both indicative of individual tragedy and suggestive of the multiple tragedies that it visually represents. We do not and cannot know the number of children who have died on precarious journeys to Europe from war-torn countries like Syria. These children's unknowability, in turn, renders their lives individually ungrievable and, thus, incapable of public reflection and political action. With this in mind, it is important to consider the potency of Alan's death as one that *was* documented and *was* grieved by global audiences who recognized its horror in conveying the reality of war and displacement. Why was this particular image so potent? And what does that potency suggest about our affective capacity to feel alongside other viewers to demand justice and social change?

When listening to this image I hear several sounds – the slow crash of the waves that brought Alan's body to shore; the short squawks of seagulls circling closely by; the constrained hum of police officers and news reporters present on the beach and stunned into near silence. Amidst this noise, I also hear silence – that silence which naturally accompanies death and temporal mourning. In viewing this image, I am mourning this little boy and the life he might have lived if things had been different. This mourning feels involuntary, as though it is a necessary part of my visual consumption. I cannot help but mourn in response to this image, and it is this reflexive response – shared by many – that holds value in its capacity to ignite social change. If European viewers respond by demanding policy reforms that would make seeking asylum safe for people like Alan when fleeing conflict zones, and if policy makers are moved to act, countless future lives could be saved. Indeed, following the release and wide circulation of Alan's photograph several European leaders *did* act by reforming their border control policies and allowing the safe passage of many Syrian refugees seeking asylum in Europe. However, when that reflexive response does not translate into meaningful political action – when it temporarily disrupts day-to-day life by offering a brief pivot away from business-as-usual – the tragic loss of life generated through this violence proliferates and countless deaths remain unrecorded and ungrieved.

This kind of disengagement further risks voyeuristic consumption, which is fundamentally apolitical. Voyeuristic consumption occurs when a private image evokes pleasure in the consumer, despite (and sometimes because of) the pain experienced by the person or people depicted in the image. Voyeuristically engaging with images of pain and suffering necessitates a fundamental disengagement with the subject as human. To see these images and gain any form of pleasure from them requires the viewer to (at least temporarily) suspend recognition of the person's humanity and perceive them as non-human. The subject is viewed as incapable of human suffering and, therefore, as incapable of feeling the pain the viewer would likely feel in their circumstances. As discussed in Chapter 3, lynching photography was popular precisely because of this affective disengagement. The lynched victim's inhumanity is both established and confirmed by their inhumane treatment before and after death, and the killers' humanity is configured by the photographic celebration of their perceived 'triumph.'

Following the release of images depicting Alan's death he was widely mourned because his death was immediately registered as a tragic loss of life. This registered loss was, in turn, predicated on Alan's relatability to global audiences with similarly aged children and the widespread association of innocence with his small, vulnerable body. Because he is a child, viewers did not typically look at Alan's body and assume he was responsible for his death, which allowed for an affective engagement with the image that called for advocacy on his behalf. Similar instances of affective engagement have been shown with other widely circulated images of suffering children. In 1993, South African photographer Kevin Carter won a Pulitzer Prize for a photograph taken during his time in Sudan, showing a young and emaciated Sudanese child seemingly on the brink of death being stalked by a nearby vulture. This photograph, named 'The Vulture and the Little Girl,' received mixed responses from viewers who both recognized its importance in increasing public attention on the famine in Sudan and saw it as a clear example of unethical photojournalism.

For those who believed the latter, Carter's decision to photograph this child's plight rather than immediately intervene and assist them signified a morally reprehensible choice to prioritize 'art' over much-needed compassion. As an adult, Carter was expected to intervene and protect this child, and his failure to do so was widely read as a decision to put his photojournalistic career before the child's life.[2] In this photo, the child is shown bent over in a foetal position with their face in their hands, their rib cage clearly visible through a thin layer of skin and their swollen stomach lightly touching the ground. The hooded vulture, positioned directly behind the child, stares intently at them, as though patiently waiting for their imminent death. The child's vulnerability is reinforced through their physical proximity to the vulture, their size (which, from the camera's angle, appears smaller than the vulture's), and their posture of seeming defeat. The whereabouts of the child's parents are unknown, and Carter is the only other person who is known to be present. Yet Carter is positioned in relation to the image – behind the camera – rather than in it, and it is this relationality that prompted public debate over the ethics of spectatorship when documenting evidence of humanitarian crises. Did Carter have an ethical obligation to immediately intervene and assist this child? Did his decision not to immediately intervene convey a seeming disregard for this child's life? How can we measure Carter's decision not to intervene against the political urgency of his work and its role in increasing global awareness of the famine he was documenting?

When analysing our affective engagement with images like this it is important for us as viewers to critically reflect on the utility of our spectatorship. If the goal of photojournalism is to reveal what is happening on the ground with the hope of prompting political discussion and/or radical change, it follows that our job as an audience is to be 'moved' by the image to the point of facilitating that goal. An ethical approach to spectatorship could, therefore, involve looking beyond the image to recognize its radical potential in mobilizing affect. The mobilization of this affect, in turn, makes clear the grievability of those whose suffering might otherwise be overlooked or dismissed as common amongst people in similar circumstances. Photographs of emaciated Black and Brown children dying from preventable causes in the Global South are commonplace in digital spaces largely occupied by people in the Global North. As such, the risk of affective desensitization is high amongst those who are inundated with images of violence that, collectively, render that violence both common and unremarkable. Following this logic, our job as viewers requires active engagement with the violent image so that it does not merely become one of many. It is only by actively engaging with the image that we in the Global North can recognize the urgency of our democratic participation, which is capable of driving much-needed change.

This engagement, however, raises important questions about the ethical implications of looking and affectively responding because of a common point of connection with the subject(s) being depicted. Images that disturb us and prompt social action often do so when they clearly convey unambiguous wrongdoing or unwarranted harm towards vulnerable people. The images of Alan's small body resonated with many parents and caregivers in Western nations who, through Alan, saw their own children. For them,

---

[2] Despite reporting that he later chased off the vulture before the child steadily stood up and made their way to the nearby feeding station they were headed to, Carter was unable to dispel this accusation throughout his career.

the political resonance of these images rested on Alan's relatability as an innocent child who could have been theirs. While one could argue that this affective relatability is natural (if a dead child resembles one's own it is, indeed, difficult to immediately suppress our responses to that relatability), it invites us to question why we must relate to these images on a personal level to grieve another's tragic circumstances. Why is it not enough to recognize and grieve a victim's loss on their own terms without our own involvement? And what does it mean for those of us in the Global North to require a level of personal engagement with those from the Global South to prompt us to act?

Saidiya Hartman succinctly outlines this conundrum when discussing how Black enslaved people gain(ed) meaning for some through their relatability to the (White) self. Hartman notes that, in the West, 'to come to any recognition of common humanity, the other must be assimilated,' which, in turn, can mean the 'other' is 'utterly displaced and effaced' in service of the viewer's 'need' to put themselves in the sufferer's shoes (Hartman and Wilderson 2003: 189). In other words, putting oneself in the sufferer's shoes causes an erasure of the subject in favour of the viewer, which can result in the viewer 'looking' at the image of another's suffering without really 'seeing' them. This looking without seeing, in turn, reinforces the idea that only certain lives are valued as such, while the 'other' is acknowledged as life only when relatable to dominant groups in positions of power.

Had Alan been older, larger, scantily dressed, bloodied or visibly mangled, the images might not have elicited the same international response, as such features could have diminished his relatability to Western audiences. By problematizing the ethics of looking I do not wish to suggest that we should *not* look or that we should turn away when presented with images of violence brought about by war and/or state policy. Rather, I want to underscore the need to reconcile the question of what it means to look with the reality of what can be done through looking. Put differently, I seek to problematize the act of looking when it is unlikely to prompt an effective response from audience members and question the perceived need to capture and circulate images of violence to make that violence known.

It is important to further consider the harms of looking for audiences who identify with the victim in ways that go beyond surface-level relatability and involve embodied experiences of living in the world. In April 2023, I visited the National Museum of African American History and Culture in Washington, DC for the second time. Starting at the bottom and moving upward through the exhibits, I was once again struck by my embodied response to standing in a replica of the hold of a slave ship, surrounded by darkness and the thunderous sound of crashing waves on either side.

Slowly making my way through the hold with the other visitors I thought, who is this exhibit for? Is it for me as a descendant of enslaved Africans who were transported to the USA through the Middle Passage, or is it for non-Black audiences whose ancestors might have directly or indirectly profited from the slave trade? If such a binary in intended audience exists, what does it mean for all of us to occupy this space together? What are the potential harms of looking and who bears the responsibility to look?

When images are reproduced for the image's sake, or when they are configured to generate shock value, they lose their affective capacity to instigate change. Moreover, when our affective responses to violent images are not sustained – when they offer fleeting recognitions of the need for change without spurring follow-up action – they risk reproducing logics of ungrievability that fail to register certain lives as lives and do not count certain deaths as deaths. Put differently, when certain images are viewed as one of many, their affective potentials often fail to translate into meaningful action, which raises questions about the ethical implications of those images and the moral obligations of spectatorship.

Existing, even temporarily, in a replication of the hold did not prompt an affective relatability in me that could be used to bring about change. Even if I had not studied the psychosocial effects of the Middle Passage as a scholar, I know about it through my family's history – I *feel it* as a person who lives in the wake of this violence. What, then, does it mean for me to witness its visceral replication? Does this witnessing risk voyeuristic consumption or is that type of consumption impossible for people who personally relate to the violence being depicted? These questions are inevitable when action does not follow consumption.

As previously mentioned, the two widely circulated images of Alan Kurdi *did* spur action among political leaders which, arguably, led to wide-scale changes. In the UK, then-prime minister David Cameron responded to the images by noting that 'as a father, [he] felt deeply moved' by them and, following increased pressure from several UK politicians, committed to providing resettlement to twenty thousand Syrian refugees over a five-year period (BBC News 2015). Two days after Alan's death, Germany agreed to open its borders to thousands of refugees who had been stranded in Hungary (Kingsley 2016). Canada promised to resettle twenty-five thousand Syrians, and European leaders created a system that would see one hundred and twenty thousand refugees landing on Greek and Italian shores relocated to other European countries (Kingsley 2016).

While any increase in humanitarian aid is laudable, critics argued that the UK response, in particular, was insufficient given the scale of the crises. Critics further noted that the initial capacity these images had to affectively engage international audiences and prompt political action did little to counter the broader anti-immigrant sentiment present in many European countries at the time of Alan's death. Indeed, fears of 'migrant invasion' were common among many who were initially moved by the images but later concerned by the European adoption of liberal resettlement policies that followed shortly after. This concern typically stemmed from the perceived threat of migrants who would require initial support from public services, potentially reducing their availability for tax-paying citizens. This mode of thinking not only overlooks the role of globalization in supporting European economies and making those services possible but also speaks to the disposability of lives that are reduced to their economic cost rather than recognized for their inherent human value. Pushback against this framing often necessitates public recognition of loss that reinforces migrant grievability through overt statements and practices, many of which centre the dead child as symbolic of national, political and moral demise.

'Looking' and aesthetic abjection

I want to return briefly to the implications of voyeuristic consumption that I mentioned earlier. Specifically, I want to focus on how they relate to the transference of subject into abject 'Other'. I have thus far argued that embedded within the practice of looking is a responsibility to act on behalf of the sufferer, and that there is a need to reflect on the moral implications of our spectatorship when we are not moved to act or when we require relatability to act. In this way, I position the act of looking as one that cannot be divorced from the discursive politics that surround the image and join Tina Campt in her call for viewers to 'listen' to images to discern their affective potentials. When that listening does not or cannot occur, when it is blocked by the empathy fatigue that often accompanies repeated exposure to images of suffering and violence, spectatorship becomes a matter of individual consumption that is, arguably, unethical. Engagement with the image at this level risks dehumanizing the 'Other' whose pain is not recognized as individual pain, but as emblematic of the pain felt by many who suffer from similar violent enactments.

The unknowability of the individual's pain, and their existence at an abstract level that only affords them recognition as far as they relate to others in a similar position, gives way to their aesthetic abjection as non-humans. The non-human, in this case, is that person whose abjection retains an aesthetic appeal to viewers who are principally engaged with their suffering at a surface level, registering only the spectacular conditions of their suffering or the 'shock value' of their circumstances. Under this gaze, the person ceases to be a person and becomes the imagined form the viewer creates on their behalf. Their individualism, agency and autonomy are lost in this rubric. They become the thing that they are assumed to be.

Recognitions of the Black body as a 'trophy', signified through lynching photographs, necessitates a re-casting of the Black body as a commodity with aesthetic value. Posing next to the slain Black body, the killers can position the victim as abject in ways that evoke both the victim's visual appeal to racist audiences and their 'non-human' status. To position the Black body as 'non-human', in turn, confers a status of ungrievability. As Butler notes, 'non-lives' cannot be lost 'and cannot be destroyed, because they already inhabit a lost and destroyed zone; they are, ontologically, and from the start, already lost and destroyed, which means that when they are destroyed in war, nothing is destroyed' (Butler 2016: xix). In accordance with this framing, the impermeability of the Black 'non-human' means they are both destroyed and undestroyable. The Black body is killed but not recognized as dead because it was not seen as living in the first place.

When describing abjection and the responses we have to the aesthetic qualities of the abject body or substance in question, Julia Kristeva argues that rejection is a primary response. By clarifying the need to separate the abject from the self through rejection, Kristeva further points to contamination as a principal fear of those aesthetic qualities. Using the example of skin that sits on the surface of milk, Kristeva notes that when it is 'presented to the eyes, or touches the lips, a spasm ensues, first at the back of the throat and then lower down in the stomach, abdomen and all the intestines; it stiffens the body, brings forth tears and bile, makes the heart palpitate and beads the forehead and hands with perspiration' (Kristeva and Lechte 1982: 126). As such, recognition of the abject generates a physiological response that signifies a rejection of that substance with the aim of separating the substance from the body. Vomiting in response to the sight, smell, touch or ingestion of the milk skin would, Kristeva suggests, convey a natural response to a substance that is deemed a pollutant.

According to Kristeva, abjection is caused by that which disturbs existing identities, systems and orders (Kristeva 1982: 4). The dead body, she notes, signifies the 'utmost abjection' because it is in direct odds with the living and, through its constitution, signifies 'the breaking down of a world that has erased its borders' (Kristeva 1982: 4). When 'seen without God and outside of science,' Kristeva argues, the dead body denotes 'death infecting life. Abject. It is something rejected from which one does not part, from which one does not protect oneself as from an object. Imaginary uncanniness and real threat, it beckons to us and ends up engulfing us' (Kristeva 1982: 4). According to this logic, unlike milk skin the dead body cannot be rejected because, through its beckoning, it engulfs the viewer. Despite attempting to reject the dead body, the viewer cannot separate themselves from it because it represents their impending fate, one that is simultaneously imagined and unimaginable. The aesthetic lure of the dead body, then, is located in its relatability to an inevitable future, one in which we are all dead. We are both afraid of and drawn to the dead body because of what it suggests about our own mortality. The dead child embodies a distinct texture of abjection – one tied to the profound loss of a future that will not be actualized.

When images of death evoke life or, more specifically, when images convey the impermeability of death being confronted by the vitality of life, we recognize abjection in its fullest form. As previously noted, the image of Alan's lifeless body lying face-down on a beach drew international attention, in part, because Alan looked as if he could be sleeping. The absence of blood or other signs of bodily trauma provokes the viewer to align this image with images of sleeping children despite knowing that Alan is dead. As a dead child whose posture simulates life, Alan exists as an abject figure whose body disturbs the viewer because it straddles modes of being that are both fundamentally oppositional and unreconcilable. Visual readings of Alan as the 'living dead,' and the outpouring of grief this reading provoked, work against Kristeva's notion that the abject is inherently repulsive and towards a recognition of the abject's potential to ignite social change. It is this social change that has the power to re-imagine ungrievable lives as grievable, worthy of protection in life and commemoration in death.

Commemorating the dead child

In 2007, when I was in sixth form college,[3] I noticed a disturbing trend among some of my teenage peers who began telling 'dead baby jokes.' These 'jokes' often elicited laughter from both the speaker and the listeners, who seemed enthralled by their

---

[3]   In the UK, a sixth form college is an educational institution where students aged 16-19 typically study for advanced qualifications, such as A-levels or vocational courses.

subversive intent to shock through the macabre and taboo subject matter. I do not remember the specific 'jokes' that were told (and I would not repeat them if I did), but I do remember being morbidly fascinated by the joker's attempt to make something fundamentally unfunny funny. What was it, I wondered, that allowed these 'jokes' to become funny to some when they were clearly unfunny in everything they described and stood for? I later realized that it was the shock value located in their transgressive 'humour.' In many cultures, stories and images of dead children have historically carried this shock value in ways that have incurred both fear and censorship. Visual images of dead children remain taboo in many Western cultures that see these images as harmful to look at because of what they signify – the tragic loss of innocent life that was unable to reach its full potential. These 'jokes,' then, demonstrate an attempt to push back against this reaction by forming a narrative that both trivializes and diminishes that harm, and suggest an alternative way of understanding child death by framing it as ordinary, mundane and open to mockery.

When understanding (un)grievability as a political project that differentiates between lives that are deemed worthy of mourning after they are lost from lives that are not, it is important to consider the commemorative practices that facilitate or, in some cases, rebuff that mourning. Telling 'dead baby jokes' – even when all babies are abstractly lumped together – undermines the mourning practices of parents and caregivers who have lost children and seek to commemorate that loss through both ritual and discourse. In attempting to render such loss humorous, those who tell these 'jokes' prioritize the perceived humour in the child's death over the affective and ethical weight of that death. In doing so, they not only fail to acknowledge the harm inherent in the act of joking but also contribute to the dehumanization of the dead child by implying that their loss is not worthy of serious recognition. This mode of 'humour', then, functions not merely as a form of transgression, but also as a form of discursive violence that erodes the child's innate human value.

The perceived innocence of the dead child often serves a protective function by shielding that child from any blame for, or culpability in, their death. However, for some racially minoritized children, racist stereotyping precludes the innocence often afforded to White children who are not subjected to this stereotyping. In 2016, the French satirical magazine Charlie Hebdo published a cartoon depicting what they saw as a potential future for Alan Kurdi – as a sex offender. This cartoon was widely believed to have been drawn in response to the infamous sexual assaults that took place on New Year's Eve 2015 in Cologne, Germany, whereby roughly one hundred women were sexually assaulted by a large group of men who eyewitnesses claimed 'looked Arab or North African' (BBC News 2016). In this cartoon Alan is shown as a young adult running behind a woman with his arms outstretched while she, looking back, screams and runs away. Alan's open mouth, pig-like snout, and wide-eyes intently focused on the woman's buttocks convey a primitive predatory stare that is at direct odds with the small, circled illustration of the recognizable image of Alan's dead body in the top left-hand corner.

Under the heading 'Migrants' the caption accompanying the image reads 'que serait devenu le petit Aylan s'il avait grandi? Tripoteur de fesses en allemagne' – 'what would have become of little Aylan if he had grown up? Butt groper in Germany.' The purposeful framing of Alan as a Syrian child who, had he reached adulthood, could have resembled the men who committed sexual assault in Cologne speaks to a broader logic of representation that coexists alongside racist stereotyping. As a migrant who would likely have been racialized in similar ways, Alan is not exempt (even in death) from the racist assumption that he would have behaved in a particular way as an adult, regardless of his individual character or moral standing. The widespread recognition of Alan's innocence, prompted by the circulation of images of his dead body, is thus revealed as both fragile and fleeting. The innocence afforded to him in death would likely not have protected him in life, particularly as he grew older in a world that so often denies such innocence to racially minoritized children. Upon its release, this cartoon received backlash from those who viewed it as a racist caricature of unfounded racist assumptions. Others understood it as a tongue-in-cheek mockery of negative tabloid perceptions of refugees. Regardless of these differing opinions, it is evident that 'humour' is intentionally deployed by the artist in response to Alan's death in ways that reify the notion that migrants like Alan are subject to mockery regardless of their tragic circumstances and notable innocence.

When the images of Alan's dead body initially entered the public sphere several news and media outlets critically discussed the ethical implications of publishing them. Conversations typically centred around what publishing these images might mean for front-page viewers who would unwittingly consume them and the broader ethics of circulating images of dead children that would knowingly disturb viewers. In *The Guardian*, the 'human tragedy, pathos and sense of heartbreak' conveyed through these images 'were weighed up against potential privacy issues and the risk of repelling the reader with indecent bluntness' (Fahey 2015). Deciding to publish both photographs of Alan, *The Guardian* placed the image of the policeman carrying Alan's lifeless body on its front page, followed by the image of Alan lying face-down and alone on the beach on the next page. The second image was featured below a caption that first warned the viewer of its explicit content. By ordering the images in this way, *The Guardian* sought to first contextualize Alan's death in relation to the broader 'Syrian migrant crisis' before showing readers the reality of that crisis for vulnerable children. The sequence in which the images appear prepares the reader for the affective impact of both. The first image, while emotionally charged, eases the viewer into the more confronting reality of the second.

What does it mean to commemorate the dead child through photography? And how can these photographs be understood as political tools that can be used to promote the grievability of the ungrievable dead? To answer these questions, it is important to consider the intentionality behind the photograph, the politics of its circulation and the discourses surrounding its framing. If a photograph is taken of a child post-mortem with the aim of recording a war crime, or if forensic photography is used to document a child's suspected murder, the meaning attached to that photograph lies in its function as evidence. While the photograph may be subject to voyeuristic consumption, its intention is to offer legal proof of wrongdoing with the aim of bringing about justice for the victim. The photograph may be circulated outside of the investigative teams for whom it was originally produced, but the original meaning located in its intention remains clear. Discourses surrounding the photograph's framing are, in turn, routinely shaped by that intention. The image exists in relation to the context in which it was produced and is limited in its capacity to take on additional meaning that is divorced from that context.

When photographs of dead children are taken to aid the grieving process – when they are consumed privately and selectively by close family members and friends – they take on different meanings. In the latter part of the nineteenth century, it was common for babies and young children to be photographed shortly after death by photographers who were employed by families specifically for that purpose. Often taken in Western contexts, these photographs served as keepsakes for bereaved families grappling with loss and searching for ways to remember the dead while continuing with their own lives. Children were frequently posed in the arms of their parents or beside siblings, dressed in clothes they might have worn and surrounded by toys they might have played with. These images sought to document a life once lived by placing the deceased within the familial setting, commemorating them as a valued member of the family even in death.

In one particularly striking image, a girl who is perhaps four or five years old is shown sitting upright in a decorative upholstered chair. She appears to be at home and is accompanied by four dolls, all of whom resemble her in clothing, hairstyle and posture. The girl's head is angled to the right, her chin tilted downwards, lightly resting on her chest. Her eyes and mouth are closed; her hair is neatly trimmed and freshly curled. She has an overall look of care that suggests she was well-looked-after, nourished and pampered in life. The photographer stands slightly to the left so that they can capture all the child's dolls in the image's frame. Her figure is encased by two decorative bows that are attached to her chair and sit on either side of her face. This child – unknown to the viewer – was evidently loved by the caregivers who raised her. Although they are not in the photograph's frame the viewer senses the caregiver's presence, as though they are looking at the child alongside them (potentially standing next to the photographer). The caregiver's love and adoration are made clear by the aesthetic adornments that are carefully placed around the child, and their pain at her passing is reflected in the child's posture and her body's purposeful simulation of life. In looking at this image, the viewer could be mistaken for thinking this child is sleeping or gently resting her eyes, perhaps worn out from an afternoon playing with her dolls. This simulation of life in death signifies an attempt to continue the child's life beyond death and commemorate her life as one that was shaped by care and devotion.

This image was commissioned and captured for the child's caregivers. The child does not benefit from the image, and it does not serve to document evidence of a brutal death. Its intention is purely commemorative and, although it now exists in the public domain, it is unlikely the child's caregivers would have intended for this image to be seen by anyone outside of their immediate family. Unlike the images of Alan Kurdi, this image does not offer political condemnation or symbolize broader injustices faced by vulnerable populations. It was not captured for a broader public. This child exists alone, and the grief that her passing generated among those who loved her is private. The discourse surrounding the framing of this image is deeply personal to this child – she played with dolls, her hair was curled, she wore pinafore dresses – and offers intended viewers a brief reprieve from sorrow by evoking joyful memories tied to her individual character. Her life is remembered through the traits that made her unique and, in this way, she is grieved as a whole person: distinctive, singular and fully known.

Not all children are granted this kind of intimate commemoration after death, and not all caregivers are given the chance to mourn their children in ways that allow them to fully grieve or even begin the grieving process. In August 2014, police officer Darren Wilson fatally shot eighteen-year-old Michael Brown in Ferguson, Missouri, sparking national protests and giving rise to the Black Lives Matter movement.[4] Michael's body lay face-down in the spot where he fell, in the middle of a public street, for four hours before being moved. During that time, countless local residents saw and photographed his body; some recorded video footage while others looked on incredulously, occasionally glancing up the street for signs of an ambulance. Michael's mother, Lezley McSpadden, learned of her son's killing from a nearby witness who took a photograph of his dead body on their phone and showed it to her. Distraught, Lezley ordered the attending officers to conceal Michael's body from public view. Michael's body was eventually covered by a white sheet, his feet were exposed and blood from his gunshot wounds continued to leak beyond the sheet's borders. Circling the parameters set around her son by the authority that killed him, Lezley looked on helplessly. She was not permitted to attend to Michael's body and could do nothing for him as his mother during those initial hours. The photographs that were taken of Michael's dead body offer a gruesome reminder of his killing and do nothing to positively commemorate his life.

Unlike the private grief the unknown girl-child's family was permitted, Michael's mother's mourning is made public through the involuntary circulation of images showing both her son's dead body and her anguish in the wake of his killing. When parents and caregivers are unable to control the capturing, circulation and narrative surrounding their dead child's image – particularly when that image becomes politically charged and gains meaning for spectators seeking to determine its broader inferences – they risk experiencing the loss of their child all over again. This loss often compels a sacrifice of their child's personhood within media landscapes. Their child is (at least temporarily) no longer recognized as an individual him/her/them but as a collective 'we' that signifies a broader racist landscape. The mothers of well-known victims of anti-Black violence are united in their grief even as their children become lost in the broader discourses that inform how their lives are publicly articulated.

Black mothers who seek to reclaim their children's lives from the (often speculative) narratives attached to those broader discourses often do so through practices that (sometimes unwittingly) adhere to respectability politics. This adherence actively promotes recognition of their child as a 'reputable' member of society who is 'worthy' of grief and public mourning. In doing so, it reifies the connection between respectability

---

[4] Black Lives Matter gained momentum in the aftermath of the vigilante killing of teenager Trayvon Martin in 2013.

and (un)deservedness by suggesting that people who present in ways that are socially read as 'respectable' are deserving of grief, sympathy and care during and after life. Adherence to this respectability politics can take many forms. Principal among them is the sharing of images that directly counter public narratives of waywardness and criminality. Photographs showing their children wearing graduation gowns and mortarboard hats are often circulated by bereaved mothers who seek to actively resist dehumanizing public assumptions about their children that closely align them with racist stereotypes. These counter images reclaim the dead body from discrediting caricatures by presenting the deceased through the eyes of their mother – the person who brought them into the world and knew them best.

As I have made clear in previous chapters, there are countless Black mothers who have had to bury their children because of the lethal consequences of anti-Black violence. The expectation that one's child will potentially face lethal harm because of this violence is constant for Black mothers who raise Black children in contexts that are both unsafe and unpredictable. In her essay 'The Condition of Black Life is One of Mourning,' Claudia Rankine writes, '[i]t would be a mistake to presume that everyone who saw the image mourned [Michael] Brown, but once exposed to it, a person had to decide whether his dead black body mattered enough to be mourned' (Rankine 2015). By locating the decision to mourn Michael's death in the individual proclivities of the spectator, Rankine situates mourning and empathy as personal choices that can be opted into if desired. In this way, Rankine indirectly challenges Butler's notion of grievability as a process that operates systemically and is embedded within geo-political rationales that seek to justify or discredit war and violence.

For Rankine, the decision to grieve when presented with the image of Black death is made by the individual who can, if they choose to, act in response. When deciding whether Michael's body 'mattered enough to be mourned,' the spectator is asked to consider both the underlying logics governing the image (one that demonstrates yet another instance of lethal anti-Black state violence) and the singular figure of Michael lying dead in the street. Presented with subsequent images of Michael's mother engaged in public and private acts of mourning – both paying tribute to her son at public demonstrations and grieving privately in ways that were unknowingly caught on camera – the spectator is invited to join her but not necessarily required to do so. The broader question of Michael's grievability at a national level thus relies on how these images are individually ingested and spewed out, and the broader repercussions that are evoked (or not) through that process.

Grieving potential life

The UK-based charity *Sands* supports families affected by pregnancy loss or the death of a baby, offering grief counselling and running community-led support groups. *Sands* also helps parents commemorate their babies by providing memory boxes. These boxes may include items the parents had already chosen for their child, alongside gifts from the charity such as knitted blankets donated by members of the public. When creating these blankets, volunteers are asked to use white wool and follow specific knitting and crochet patterns that can be downloaded from the charity's website. Each memory box typically also contains a hand- and footprint kit, a baby details book, a birth certificate and two small toys, all carefully prepared before being sent to bereaved parents (Sands 2024). By seeking handcrafted donations from volunteers, *Sands* not only encourages public support for the charity's initiative but also actively involves the public in a commemorative practice that seeks to both reify life and acknowledge death. By participating in this commemorative practice, the volunteer actively supports the grieving parent by anonymously sharing their grief in ways that make it public. Their labour expresses solidarity with the parent through a communal recognition of their loss and a commitment to mark their loss as shared.

For parents who lose their children through miscarriage or stillbirth, grieving can take on multiple meanings that incorporate both loss of potential life (imagining who their child might have been) and a recalibration of the parents' role as primary caregiver and child-rearer. Because they are no longer able to raise their children, parents may grieve the loss of that role alongside the loss of their children. For some parents, reckoning with this layered grief may involve creating public memorials for their child, establishing endowments in their name or privately commemorating milestones such as birthdays. Through these acts, the child is shown to 'live' in the present through their ongoing legacy.

Groups referring to themselves as 'pro-life' or 'anti-abortion' typically locate the beginning of life at the point of conception, equating the ending of that life at any point with the ending of human life. This position, typically adopted by conservatives and those on the political Right, humanizes the foetus as an 'unborn baby' with human rights and entitlements. Terms like 'pro-life' are often used to suggest that taking an anti-abortion stance works in favour of life by 'saving babies' from premature death. At the time of writing, several US campaigns and organizations exist to implement this notion through direct intervention in pregnancy clinics, often situating their arguments in relation to Christian teachings and biblical rhetoric. PreBorn!, a non-profit Christian organization based in Indianapolis, Indiana, offers support to what they describe as 'life-affirming' pregnancy clinics by providing them with ultrasound equipment, counselling services and educational materials for pregnant people (PreBorn! 2024). According to PreBorn!'s website, their aim in providing these resources is to 'surround each abortion-seeking woman with a network of care that makes it possible for her to choose life – and life in Christ.' By providing a 'network of care,' the group's hope is that the pregnant person comes to realize the 'correct' decision for them and their foetus, which is to continue with their pregnancy (to 'choose life') and to develop a relationship with God. This relationship will, in turn, guide them as parents and provide the emotional support they need to 'parent well'.

Stories about pregnant people who have been influenced by PreBorn!'s targeted advertising routinely focus on the impact of their ultrasound scan in their decision to 'choose life.' By seeing the foetus move and interact on screen, prospective parents argue that the ultrasound provides an opportunity to witness life by showing foetal characteristics that are compatible with human life (for example, physical movement). 'Witnessing the life' of the foetus, in turn, facilitates the prospective parent's decision to 'save life' rather than 'end' it, and in doing so enables their conformity to Christian beliefs that seek to preserve human life and ensure human protection. In this way, reproductive technologies such as ultrasound screenings that facilitate pathways towards preserving foetal life offer an effective tool in promoting moral doctrines that, on the surface, oppose death and seek to make potential life grievable. One of the stories PreBorn! use, titled 'The Ultrasound That Revealed Truth,' is worth quoting at length,

> Eissa wanted to confirm her pregnancy, so she went in for an ultrasound at a PreBorn! Network Clinic while her boyfriend, Damian, waited outside. They were planning a trip to Louisiana for an out-of-state abortion when they found the Clinic, which was just across the street from Eissa's college in Houston. Miraculously, they noticed the building for the first time.
>
> She was astonished and deeply moved when the ultrasound revealed beautiful, identical twins. She called Damian, 'Come inside, NOW!'
>
> Although he was reluctant, Damian eventually confronted the truth he couldn't deny. Faced with his babies' lives right in front of him, he wept. Eissa, Damian and the ultrasound technician watched in amazement as the twins interacted with each other, already closely bonded. Despite being early in her pregnancy, Eissa's little babies were full of personality and sucking each other's toes.
>
> The two strong parents were so moved by this powerful encounter, that they decided to cancel their trip to Louisiana.
>
> Damian said he was a believer, but he was so afraid of becoming a dad. He found an encouraging ally in one of the male volunteers. By the end of their visit, Eissa and Damian rededicated their lives to Jesus, laying down their burdens and fears at His feet, and trusting God with their twin babies.
>
> (PreBorn! 2023: 11)

The moment at which this story begins – with Eissa knowing about the pregnancy and seeking confirmation of it – offers an optimal point of intervention for PreBorn! who aim to persuade against abortion by presenting what they perceive as the 'truth' of the image on screen at a time when a final decision has not yet been made. By showing the couple an image of both foetuses seemingly interacting with each other on screen, the ultrasound makes visible and substantive that which was previously invisible and abstract. By revealing the shape and form of the foetuses, these images appeal to what Catherine Mills describes as the 'sympathetic imagination,' wherein the foetus is imagined as a suffering being that can experience human pain. This imagining, Mills argues, is made possible because 'the foetal life exposed in the ultrasound image is one that we have all lived through. Each of us has already been a foetus, and we come to understand that a foetus "is" a being capable of suffering because we are capable of suffering' (Mills 2011: 107). According to Mills, by recognizing the foetus as a former 'us' we imagine ourselves in the place of the foetus and, consequently, reconfigure the foetus as worthy of protection from harm. This logic not only overlooks the biological relativity of the foetus in question but also raises the moral question – discussed earlier – of whether relatability should be a prerequisite for empathy.

The 'pro-life'/anti-abortion push to humanize the foetus through ultrasound images that seemingly evoke life purposefully aligns the foetus with young infants whose vulnerability is indisputable. The perceived vulnerability of the foetus, created through and sustained by its ascribed innocence, reinforces the belief that the foetus should be protected by those with the power to do so. In this way, the foetus is presented as grievable by those who argue that its 'life' holds human value and that the destruction of that 'life' is equivalent to the destruction of human life. By encouraging parent–child bonding through foetal ultrasound imaging, proponents commonly argue that they are acting on behalf of the sufferer (in this case, the foetus) and are giving voice to the voiceless (the 'pre-born infant'). In recent years, several US states have required ultrasound imaging to be completed prior to abortion and for pregnant people to be given the option of viewing these images. In 2008, Oklahoma went one step further by making it mandatory for pregnant people to be shown the ultrasound images and have them explained before seeking an abortion (Mills 2011: 109).

For pregnant people who do not wish to see these images or know of their contents, this forced subjection can generate harm despite its purported intent to reduce harm to both the foetus (in 'preserving life') and the pregnant person (in helping them make the 'right decision'). The violence embedded in this forced spectatorship requires a re-figuring of what it means to be vulnerable, calling into question the pregnant person's susceptibility to harm even as the act that brings it about purports to reduce that susceptibility by providing what is framed as 'support'. By offering 'support' to the pregnant person through so-called 'positive guidance', proponents overlook the myriad ways in which that guidance risks compromising the pregnant person's mental health by encouraging them to continue with a pregnancy that could jeopardize their future well-being. Despite claiming that these images reveal the objective 'truth' of the 'pre-born' foetus, they cannot be divorced from the discursive politics that surround them, nor can they be understood outside of the clinical framings that govern them. Through the political impetus informing their circulation, these images privilege the grievability of the perceived innocent (the foetus) over the well-being of the perceived culpable (the pregnant person), thereby mobilizing the spectacle of the 'dead child' in service of a moral project that directs 'care' towards lives deemed valuable.

References

BBC News. (2015), 'David Cameron: UK to accept "thousands" more Syrian refugees', https://bbc.co.uk/news/uk-34148913 (accessed 29 September 2024).

BBC News. (2016), 'Cologne attacks: New Year's Eve crime cases top 500', https://www.bbc.co.uk/news/world-europe-35277249 (accessed 29 September 2024).

Butler, J. (2016), *Frames of War: When Is Life Grievable?* Verso.

Campt, T. (2017), *Listening to Images*. Duke University Press.

Fahey, J. (2015), 'The Guardian's decision to publish shocking photos of Aylan Kurdi,' *The Guardian*, https://www.theguardian.com/commentisfree/2015/sep/07/guardian-decision-to-publish-shocking-photos-of-aylan-kurdi (accessed 29 September 2024).

Hartman, S. and F. B. Wilderson. (2003), 'The Position of the Unthought', *Qui Parle*, 13 (2): 183–201.

Kingsley, P. (2016), 'The death of Alan Kurdi: One Year On, Compassion towards Refugees Fades,' *The Guardian*, https://www.theguardian.com/world/2016/sep/01/alan-kurdi-death-one-year-on-compassion-towards-refugees-fades (accessed 29 September 2024).

Kristeva, J. (1982), *Powers of Horror: An Essay on Abjection*. Columbia University Press.

Kristeva, J. and J. Lechte. (1982), 'Approaching Abjection', *Oxford Literary Review*, 5 (1–2): 125–49.

Linfield, S. (2010), *The Cruel Radiance: Photography and Political Violence*. University of Chicago Press.

Mills, C. (2011), *Futures of Reproduction: Bioethics and Biopolitics*. Springer.

PreBorn! (2023), 'Annual Report', https://preborn.com/finance (accessed 29 September 2024).

PreBorn! (2024), https://preborn.com (accessed 29 September 2024).

Rankine, C. (2015), 'The Condition of Black Life is One of Mourning', *The New York Times*, https://www.nytimes.com/2015/06/22/magazine/the-condition-of-black-life-is-one-of-mourning.html (accessed 29 September 2024).

Sands. (2024), https://www.sands.org.uk/support-you/how-we-offer-support/memory-box (accessed 29 September 2024).

Conclusion

Imagining Grievable Futures

Throughout this book, I have argued for the need to disentangle the relationship between grievability and notions of individual responsibility in the context of racially minoritized health outcomes. I have also emphasized the importance of examining how and why empathy is extended to some and withheld from others, and the role of the spectator in shaping those logics when assessing contemporary patterns, expressions and modes of grievability. Problematically, our ability to position ourselves in relation to the sufferer – whether slowly dying under the knee of a police officer, languishing in a Syrian detention camp, gaining weight to reduce the risk of sexual violence, enduring prolonged solitary confinement or drowning during a perilous sea crossing while fleeing war and conflict – often determines not only how, when and why empathy is extended, but also to whom. This empathy can be pivotal in shaping the distribution of humanitarian aid, the lobbying for and enactment of legal reforms, the reach and framing of public health messaging, and the deadly consequences of restrictive border policies.

At the time of writing, riots have erupted across the UK following the murder of three young girls who were killed while attending a Taylor Swift-themed dance class in Southport, Merseyside. The rioters, who are overwhelmingly White men, have primarily targeted mosques and hotels known to house refugees and asylum seekers following online rumours that the killer was a Muslim asylum seeker. In response to these riots, law officials decided to release the name of the seventeen-year-old killer – Axel Rudakubana – to quell targeted violence towards Muslim groups. The presumptive hope these decision-makers had was that learning Rudakubana was born and raised in Wales would de-escalate tension among the British Far-Right whose anger routinely stems from age-old beliefs about 'migrant invasions' and Muslim extremism. However, in the days following the public release of Rudakubana's name riots escalated, and hotels known to house refugees remained the target of violent aggression. One could argue that the hope that learning Rudakubana is neither a refugee nor a Muslim would dissipate the riots was naïve. Although British, Rudakubana is Black and the child of Rwandan migrants and this, for some, mitigates the truth of his British citizenship and the ostensible value that privilege affords him. He is, to quote journalist Afua Hirsch, 'Brit(ish)' (Hirsch 2018) and the fact of his Blackness is indicative of his 'foreignness' to those who consider whiteness synonymous with Britishness, and who are willing to temporally extend Brit(ish)ness to racially minoritized groups when they conform to characteristics and behaviours caught up in this synonymity.

When watching videos of these Far-Right groups setting large, wheeled objects alight and ramming them into hotels with the hope of harming or, at the very least, instilling fear in the refugees housed inside them I am struck by the irony of these actions. These groups claim to be acting in response to the murder of three innocent children who were set upon by a person unknown to them while participating in a dance class. Yet the refugees who are on the receiving end of this violence include innocent children who are being attacked by persons unknown to them while playing, eating, interacting and – possibly – dancing in their provided homes. The violence directed towards these children and their families, none of whom have any connection to Rudakubana, symbolizes the ever-present threat of violence migrant families face in societies that refuse to see them as grievable and are quick to advocate in favour of their disposal when they are seen as a 'threat' to politically legitimized citizens. These children are not afforded the same thought, care, or respect the three children who were tragically murdered were because their existence is understood within the context of their position as refugees by proxy of their parents' status. Unlike the images of Alan Kurdi that evoked sympathy and affective care, these children remain faceless.

What would it mean for all lives to be considered grievable, and how might this utopic idea gain traction in a world that is governed by entrenched political determinations of lives that matter and lives that do not? This question is the subject of this final chapter, which moves from recognitions of contemporary logics of grievability to imagining grievable futures. By taking seriously these utopic possibilities, I discuss ways of imagining grievable futures through productive anti-racist action and highlight private and communal ways of promoting grievability by attending to the question of liveable life. Moving beyond strategies that facilitate *existence* in racist environments, I ask how Black and Brown life can be – and is – cultivated in ways that enable *thriving* in those environments. In other words, I consider how Black and Brown people might move beyond mere strategies of survival to enacting strategies for living. This involves, among other things, celebrating the attributes that have historically marked us as ungrievable and reckoning with our ability to self-actualize.

In this chapter, I take as a starting point the following question asked by bell hooks in her book *Sisters of the Yam: Black Women and Self-Recovery*, '[w]hat would it mean for black people to collectively believe that despite racism and other forces of domination we can find everything that we need to live well in the universe, including the strength to engage in the kind of political resistance that can transform domination?' (hooks 2015: 46). In asking this question, hooks prompts us to consider ways of existing – and resisting – within the very systems that seek to suppress our lives, as well as ways of 'living well' while advocating for necessary changes. Central to living well, hooks argues, is our ability to cultivate the strength that is needed to continue fighting for alternative anti-racist futures. Without that strength, hooks suggests, we cannot transform current systems of domination. Finding 'everything that we need to live well in the universe' involves re-evaluating and/or reminding ourselves of the resources that provide us with sustenance while we do this work. It is a reminder that those resources exist and can be used for this purpose if utilized efficiently, as well as a call to find other ways of living that are self-actualized and self-reliant. If we can locate and utilize these resources ourselves, hooks suggests, we can sustain our energy whilst participating in anti-racist activism and partaking in different forms of anti-racist action. This sustenance allows us to imagine grievable futures by actively facilitating our ability to dream and envision alternative ways of being. Without that ability, we may not know how to act or what to do when confronted with the harsh realities that existing structures and systems present us with.

There is a tension between the need for self-actualization and self-sustenance and the need for systemic political change. The former involves independent work that serves a protective function when enacted effectively, while the latter involves collective work to overhaul current systems, structures and institutions that promote harm. When it comes to independent work in the service of anti-racist action, it is important to consider the cost of that work to the individual and to consider its sustainability among those who grow tired of fighting and self-soothing. Maintaining the level of resilience that is needed to combat everyday racism is not an easy feat for those who are constantly burdened by the harms it generates. As we have seen in previous chapters, the daily grind of withstanding, swallowing and learning to live with racism can have negative effects on Black and Brown health and well-being. This grind (often theorized within the context of 'weathering') and its associated chronic stress can increase one's risk of developing numerous stress-related health conditions including hypertension, muscle pain, cancer and anxiety. In this way, maintaining resilience can reinforce a double burden of racism, requiring those who experience it to manage both the racism itself and their individual responses to it.

For those who cultivate individual resilience while simultaneously working towards anti-racist change, resilience is often construed as a temporary 'stop gap' – a remedial measure within the broader struggle for racial justice. In this framing, the remedy lies in the practices, observances and/or connections that provide respite from the ongoing presence of racism, enabling people to better cope with its daily harms. When living in unjust societies, it is important to enact optimal modes of living when confronted with everyday forms of violence that seek to diminish self-worth and promote racialized (un)grievability. By optimal modes of living, I refer to daily acts that can determine our ability to thrive in contexts that directly and indirectly suppress our lives, and to ways of being that directly contradict racist denigration. Within this framework, acts of self-care function as acts of self-preservation, carrying political weight through the value they affirm at an individual level. As poet and Black feminist Audre Lorde reminds us, caring for oneself 'is not self-indulgence, it is self-preservation, and that is an act of political warfare' (Lorde 1988). In this chapter, I offer personal reflections on how joy and beauty can be mobilized in the service of anti-racist action, providing alternative practices that cultivate resilience while advancing systemic change. In doing so, I argue that both can offer tactics for optimal living that foster grievability when it is denied by affirming humanity in the face of racist violence and denigration.

Beauty as anti-racist method

In her book *Ordinary Notes*, Christina Sharpe reflects on her mother's cultivation of beauty as a response to the conditions of daily life in an anti-Black world. This cultivation took place at home and proffered a recognition of Blackness that was oriented around care, delicacy and affective pleasure. Sharpe writes,

> Knowing that every day that I left the house, many of the people whom I encountered did not think me precious and showed me so, my mother gave me space to be precious – as in vulnerable, as in cherished. It is through her that I first learned that beauty is a practice, that beauty is a method, and that a vessel is also 'a person into whom some quality (such as grace) is infused' … My mother gave me space to dream. For whole days at a time, she left me with and to words, curled up in a living room windowsill, uninterrupted in my reading and imagining other worlds.
>
> (Sharpe 2023: 80-5)

For Sharpe, her mother's permission and facilitation of her innate vulnerability provided respite from the racism she encountered outside her home through its aim of fostering her emotional and spiritual growth. By providing Sharpe with a space to be precious and vulnerable Sharpe's mother instilled in her an understanding of the need for both when surrounded by anti-Black thought, rhetoric and violence. Without this space, Sharpe suggests, she would likely have been ill-equipped to withstand the everyday violence she encountered from those who did not see her as precious, vulnerable or worthy of being cherished. In this way, the beauty that Sharpe's mother enacted in this space offered Sharpe armament against the negative impact of those encounters. By equipping her with tools for self-actualization, Sharpe's mother facilitated her ability to counter denigrating and debilitating ideas of what it means to be a little Black girl in a racist society that failed to recognize her as innately grievable. In addition, by giving her 'space to dream,' Sharpe's mother allowed her to envision alternative realities that directly countered her lived experience and made room for imaginings of alternative anti-racist futures.

The images that accompany Sharpe's text consist of a handwritten list showing her mother's ornate handwriting, a childhood dress her mother carefully stitched for her with purple, lilac and blue appliqué tulips, and her mother's delicately crafted Christmas ornaments. The care and attention to detail that went into creating each item is made clear by her mother's embellished stitching, mindful symmetry and ornamental placing. To look at these items and see these details is to recognize the practical application of maternal affection. Sharpe's dress, in particular, speaks to the ways in which cultivating beauty can emblematize maternal care. The ornamental and distinctly feminine nature of this dress – from its colours to its patterns to its shape – conveys Sharpe's mother's desire for her daughter to know that she is loved, revered and cherished. Through their positioning in a book that provides notes on Black ordinary life – one that is routinely marred by violence, hatred and denigration – these items call attention to the need to recognize Black life as synonymous with beauty and its attendant inferences of care, nurturance and cultivation. Black life is shaped by more than the racism that polices it, this book suggests; it is also shaped by ordinary modes of living that cling to beauty for its aesthetic value alone. This aesthetic value is universally sought by people who derive pleasure from observing and/or creating beauty, and can be found in multiple sources that adorn living environments, cultural sites and bodily landscapes. This aesthetic value can also be life-affirming. It reminds the observer that, while Black existence might be shaped by denigration, it is not defined by it.

When it is used in the service of anti-racist action, beauty can offer ways of re-thinking what it means to actively promote anti-racism through private work. Like many Black girls growing up in predominantly White environments, I used to see my hair as a problem in need of fixing. My 'too big' textured hair was at odds with that of the other girls in my class who wore theirs in neat single braids and ponytails, and it did not align with the popularized straight flat hair aesthetic of the early 2000s. When I first got my hair chemically relaxed at the age of fourteen I was euphoric, not because I liked the way I looked with straight hair but because my hair finally allowed me to embody a look shared by my classmates. I received compliments from White peers at school who positively appraised my efforts to conform and was devastated when, at the end of the week, my hair returned to a curly state after washing. The hair straightening iron that my mother purchased for me was unable to return my hair to its former straight flat glory, and I now had to contend with big straight(ish) hair that frizzed with the slightest hint of rain. I chemically relaxed my hair intermittently between the ages of fourteen and eighteen but mostly wore it in a low bun at the nape of my neck to hide any visible detection of frizz. I was both embarrassed and ashamed of my hair in ways that, to this day, fill me with deep sadness and an overwhelming sense of unease.

When I turned eighteen and left home for university I made a conscious decision to stop straightening my hair. I grew out the remaining chemical relaxer and experimented with the curly hair products that were slowly emerging in retail outlets across rural parts of the UK. I also, eventually, started wearing my hair down in public. This process, and the need for it, arose at a time in my life when I was largely unaware of how anti-Black racism had shaped my life up until that point. I did it because I instinctively recognized a need to cultivate my natural hair to feel inner peace with who I was and what I looked like in a world that failed to affirm either. Today, the weekly act of tending to my hair – from washing and conditioning it to carefully styling and diffusing it – continues that work of anti-racist unlearning by requiring me to engage in a beauty practice that necessitates care, patience and devoted time. When I do this work, I am reminded of its political gravitas and the ways in which self-care can offer ratifying armament against the entrenched normalization of anti-Blackness. I self-actualize beauty as an anti-racist method by cultivating a trait that I was previously made to believe was unattractive and, therefore, problematic. I mobilize self-care through hair care as a private anti-racist act with politically affirming implications.

When seen in others, acts such as this routinely signal that person's care for their appearance in ways that may or may not register as anti-racist praxis. It is not the case that all Black women and girls choose to wear their hair naturally for self-actualizing anti-racist reasons, nor is it the case that all Black women and girls who continue to straighten their hair do so because they are ashamed of their natural hair. While these individual acts are directly shaped by the societies that promote them, they are not necessarily the outcome of that generative process. Regardless of the intention, when Black and Brown people live and interact in predominantly White spaces and engage in normative beauty practices for self-affirming reasons those practices cannot be divorced from the standardization of White beauty norms. To do so would overlook the myriad interruptions that routinely disrupt self-affirming ideas of natural Black and Brown beauty and would fail to account for everyday efforts to withstand those interruptions.

In Western neoliberal contexts that routinely distribute grievability along racialized lines, beauty practices that signal care, love and attention can be understood as radical acts that purposefully resist that uneven distribution. By implementing these beauty practices, people who fall into this category offer ways of challenging racist ideas of who is grievable and who is not by presenting ourselves as worthy of care and attention. In other words, by attending to our physical appearance through these beauty practices we inadvertently (and sometimes deliberately) offer a response to negative associations between racialized appearance markers and ungrievability that purposefully undermines those logics. Beauty, in this sense, becomes a method for resisting ungrievability.

When it comes to beautiful 'things' or ornaments that exist in private spaces, their arrangement, placement and preservation can be understood as ways to 'make pretty' that which might otherwise be (at best) plain or (at worst) unliveable. Attending to the plainness/unliveability of one's home – marking it as one's own by lacing it with decorative objects, some of which hold sentimental value and others that are merely there for aesthetic reasons – holds different meanings for different people. Home ownership, and the status that often accompanies it, has historically been viewed as aspirational by Black Americans who were (and are) prevented from purchasing their own home because of structural racism, which includes (amongst other things) red-lining policies and a comparative lack of inter-generational wealth. For those who are able to purchase their own homes, adornment can function as a private practice that marks, celebrates and solidifies home ownership and its attending social significance. In writing this I am reminded of Toni Morrison's novel *The Bluest Eye*, and the retrospective rationale Claudia gives for the numerous decorative objects that were (and are) commonly seen in the homes of Black homeowners,

> Propertied black people spent all their energies, all their love, on their nests. Like frenzied, desperate birds, they overdecorated everything; fussed and fidgeted over their hard-won homes; canned, jellied, and preserved all summer to fill the cupboards and shelves; they painted, picked, and poked at every corner of their houses. And these houses loomed like hothouse sunflowers among the rows of weeds that were the rented houses.
>
> (Morrison 2007: 18)

'Fussing', 'fidgeting' and 'overdecorating' allow the owner to stamp their property with signs of ownership that mark their achievement, while distinguishing it from rented properties that do not permit the symbolic value associated with such adornment. It is both a way of acknowledging success despite the multiple barriers that have made that success unlikely and a way of carving out space that enables self-expression and the creation of a nurturing environment.

In writing this, I am reminded of my own grandmother's house in Arkansas, which was decorated with ostentatious (though inexpensive) ornaments that conventionally signal wealth, status and success. In the formal living room – one we children were only permitted to enter for a few short hours on Christmas Day under the watchful eye of adults – was a large imposing chandelier that hung low over the dining room table. Even though few people ever entered this room (the living was primarily done in the small informal seating area off the kitchen) the table was always neatly set with silver eating utensils, placemats and napkins resting delicately on a large pink tablecloth. There was always a decorative centrepiece of some kind containing dried flowers or some other floral embellishment. On the rare occasion that the door to this room was open my brother, cousins and I looked inside and wondered at its grandeur. Its purpose was to be observed and appreciated for its aesthetic value alone and my grandmother carefully preserved it to maintain that purpose. It was a signal – a demonstration – of my grandmother's success in building this space for herself, one where she could experience, cultivate and enjoy beauty at her leisure. It was inadvertently created in response to the racism and poverty she experienced before she could create this space. It antithesized that ugliness.

At its core, beauty as an anti-racist method is a humanizing project that highlights the multiple uses of beauty in fostering care and resilience among marginalized groups. It is a survival strategy for those burdened by the harms of everyday racism, and a way to extend protection to others who are similarly burdened by it. As Christina Sharpe shows us, it is a way of knowing and communicating maternal love that extends beyond attending to physical needs and encompasses paths towards spiritual and emotional liberation. When it comes to questions of grievability, beauty as an anti-racist method offers a way to demonstrate innate value through self-cultivation. By critically attending to myself, I am presenting myself as worthy of that critical attention, and by providing myself with a private environment that fosters my well-being through beauty I am presenting my well-being as a priority. In both instances, I am actively doing grievability work by fostering my ability to withstand the racist denigration that tells me I am less worthy of care and less grievable than my peers. I am also doing grievability work by challenging the assumption that I routinely view my existence as a racially minoritized person in relation to my subjugation. By indulging in objects, well-being practices and spaces that bring me joy because of their aesthetic qualities alone, and by engaging in beauty practices that visually reflect the care I have chosen to invest in myself, I am actively resisting the pervasive threat of violence, fear and abjection that is rooted in racist ideology and action.

Black joy as anti-racist method

In the summer of 2020, Black people across the world succumbed to feelings of grief, despair and hopelessness after George Floyd was publicly murdered by White police officer Derek Chauvin in Minneapolis, Minnesota. Media coverage of this brutal killing was both descriptive and gruesome, with several high-profile media outlets circulating images and video footage of the murder online. Since then, several high-profile killings of Black people by police officers have been videoed and circulated in similar ways and have generated similar responses. At the time of writing, the most recent high-profile police killing is that of Sonya Massey on 6 July 2024. Massey was a Black 36-year-old mother with paranoid-schizophrenia living in Springfield, Illinois, who was killed by police officer Sean Grayson after calling the police because she suspected someone was trying to break into her home. When Grayson and his partner entered Massey's home, Grayson told Massey to remove a pot of boiling water from the stove to avoid starting a fire. When handling the pot as instructed, Massey said 'I'll rebuke you in the name of Jesus' before attempting to kneel behind the counter with her hands up. Massey apologized for her remark twice whilst Grayson advanced towards her. She was then fatally shot three times, at least once in the head.

Killings such as this that lay bare the perceived disposability of Black life, particularly when that life is conditioned by lived experience of mental illness, routinely prompt engagement with visual content that publicly humanizes Black people through articulations of Black joy. In their book *The Black Joy Project: A Literary and Visual Love Letter to How We Thrive*, Kleaver Cruz details a project they initiated in 2015 that centres Black joy. This project emerged from Cruz's response to the anti-racist, TLGBQIA+ and transnational solidarity work they were doing, which routinely exposed them to pain and suffering and led to a deterioration in their health and well-being. Cruz created *The Black Joy Project* to resist anti-Black racism through positive affirmations of Black life, creativity, autonomy and subjecthood in ways that directly counter anti-Black subjection. Their rationale for this project is worth quoting at length:

[T]oward the end of that year, in late November, I woke up sad in the corner room of the sixth-floor walk-up apartment in the Bronx that I shared with my twin brother and his partner. It was a morning I wished I hadn't woken up at all. On a spiritual, physical, and mental level, I was frozen. My grief that morning was overwhelming, and I felt more depressed than I had ever felt. I was stuck, in every sense of the word. I could not physically get out of bed, so I stared at the ceiling and tried to make sense of what was different about that day and why. Eventually, I had what can only be described as a spiritual experience: I felt a sudden rush of memories come over me in the middle of all the grief and other challenges I was processing from the year. They practically flashed above my head like a projector showing a movie. I saw scenes of laughter with the people I loved after a challenging day of work; long threads of funny GIFs and heart emojis in group texts with comrades and close friends; two people dear to me getting married in the middle of Prospect Park in Brooklyn, surrounded by their loving community; hugs from my loved ones during that first season of holidays without my uncle. Then the words 'Black' and 'Joy' seemed to float in front of me, so clear and so close that I could nearly touch them … Since 2015, The Black Joy Project has become both a real-world and a digital movement that amplifies joy and affirms it as a form of resistance to all that works to eliminate our joy.

(Cruz 2023: 8-10)

Caught in a moment of emotional, spiritual and physical 'stuckness', Cruz felt impulsively oriented towards Black joy as a way of becoming unstuck through communal healing. This healing was made possible by Cruz's memories of loved ones experiencing and bestowing joy, as well as their ability to recognize the underlying significance of that conglomeration. For Cruz, Black joy initially served a medicinal purpose by alleviating symptoms of grief and depression and offering alternative representations of Blackness that contradict and confront negative characterizations of Black life. Through Black joy, Cruz could see beyond anti-Black violence and Black death to envision the emancipatory possibilities of Black life – possibilities that are driven and sustained by alternative dreams of Black liberation.

The stories and artworks depicted in *The Black Joy Project* offer reflections on the healing potentials of Black joy. The affirming impact of positive representation is conveyed through artistic and real-life portrayals of Black people smiling, laughing, dancing, loving and celebrating themselves and each other. This aesthetic does not come from a proscribed adherence to respectability politics, which might show Black people enacting the above within strict framings that characterize them as demure, conservative, status-conscious or assimilationist to garner interracial approval. Rather, it comes from an organic recognition of what brings genuine joy to people who live within and despite the confines of racist structures and systems. As Cruz suggests, Black joy can be understood as a political orientation with protective health benefits. Positive health behaviours that are commonly associated with Black joy, such as dancing and consuming wholesome foods, can potentially improve health by decreasing disease risk and increasing overall well-being. Additionally, participating in Black joy activities, such as creative writing and other forms of artistic practice can boost self-esteem and increase feelings of empowerment. This can, in turn, lead to an uptake in health affirming self-care practices. In this way, Black joy can be understood as a positive resource that promotes racial health equity through tailored action.

It could be argued that the joy depicted through Cruz's project is, at its root, universal. Spending time with friends and family, dancing with a romantic partner, lovingly tending to one's children or finding moments of stillness in natural surroundings are experiences that many people find joyful. But what differentiates joy from Black joy, Cruz suggests, is the radical potential of witnessing and self-actualizing Black peoples' joy on Black peoples' terms. In other words, the difference lies in how Black joy is forged by and for Black people who regularly endure denigration, violence and other forms of suffering. It also lies in Black joy's refusal to adhere to prescriptive notions of what Blackness is and its embrace of what Black joy means to the people who embody it. Black joy is not a monolithic concept because Black people are not a monolith, and its variability – shown through how it is differentially expressed – adds to its political significance by offering holistic conceptions and interpretations of Black life.

Not every person who experiences Black joy concurrently thinks about anti-Black racism. Nor is Black joy always consumed in ways that offer relief from anti-Black violence. Indeed, one of the central commitments of Black joy is to centre Black people's jubilation on their own terms and without the intrusion of others for whom it is not designed or intended. Yet Black joy is inherently political. Popularized online in response to the global reckoning with systemic anti-Blackness in 2020, Black joy is rooted in social and political conditions that make it a vital resource for Black people seeking self-affirmation and respite from anti-Black violence. Historically, its significance has emerged in political movements and moments of violent subjugation where its expression was vital.

While the term Black joy has been popularized in recent years to describe affirmative responses to Black life that purposefully counter instances of anti-Black violence, Black joy has always existed and has always underpinned Black life, even if only expressed privately. Throughout history, Black people have resisted the dehumanization imposed on them by the Transatlantic Slave Trade, Jim Crow laws, Apartheid and other racist systems by engaging in joyful practices that are purposefully self-affirming. These practices have included singing, cooking, sharing food, reading, dancing, creative writing, volunteering, creating and listening to music and storytelling among others. When discussing her childhood in the all-Black town of Eatonville, Florida, novelist Zora Neale Hurston described her joy in singing and dancing for both the White and Black people who would pass through her town, often in exchange for cash (Hurston 2023). While these acts might now be (and often were then) seen as ones that risk reinforcing racist stereotypes – such as the 'happy darky,' who is portrayed as content with their subjugation and unwilling to challenge the status quo – for Hurston, they signified genuine enjoyment beyond the confines of these stereotypes and their limitations. Hurston sang and danced because these acts brought her joy and cared little for how they were interpreted by others. As such, these acts can be understood as ones that directly evoke Black joy through their centring of the inclinations and responses of the Black actor.

Despite Hurston's insistence on enacting Black joy even when it inadvertently propagates racist stereotypes, when it comes to understanding Black joy as an anti-racist method that slippage is arguably significant. If the aim of using Black joy as an anti-racist method is to challenge dehumanizing depictions of Black life that reduce it to experiences of suffering and abjection, reinforcing dehumanizing stereotypes that refute holistic understandings of Black life risks countering that aim. In other words, by inadvertently reinforcing racist stereotypes, Black people who do so arguably risk working against anti-racist efforts to present Black life in holistic terms. Although Hurston directly rejects the assumption that her life is characterized by abjection simply because she is Black – indeed, in her essay 'How it Feels to be Colored Me' Hurston presents Black life as somewhat advantageous because it is not governed by the rigid expectations that govern White life (Hurston 2023) – critics routinely chastize her seeming conformity to racist clichés and often denote its regressive implications. Fellow novelist Richard Wright denigrated Hurston's novel *Their Eyes Were Watching God* by noting that she 'voluntarily continues in her novel the tradition which was forced upon the Negro in theatre, that is, the minstrel technique that makes "white folk" laugh' (Ward and Butler 2008: 37). While commending Hurston's lyricism, Wright argues against what he views as Hurston's flattened, simplistic and stereotypical characterizations of Black life that routinely convey Black joy in its myriad representations. These characterizations, Wright argues, are created by and for White audiences, thereby placing them outside the conventional parameters of Black joy.

For critics like Wright, artistic characterizations of Black life that seemingly adhere to racist stereotypes should be met with political resistance that challenges the conditions producing those characters. Rather than celebrating them on their own terms, Wright suggests through his characterization of figures such as Bigger Thomas in *Native Son* that these depictions should be interpreted in relation to the contexts that give them (negative) meaning. In this framework, Black joy expressed through such characters is reduced to an acknowledgement of Black abjection. Unlike Wright, Hurston views presenting Black life in all its myriad forms and celebrating Black traditions that might be seen as primitive to people who are not Black as important ways to convey what it means to be Black. Rather than focusing on what White people might think about her characters, Hurston's goal is to communicate the holistic nature of Black life and the joy it contains to readers who may or may not identify with it.

At its root, Black joy can be understood as a way of challenging systems, structures and institutions that render Black life ungrievable by reducing it to a unilateral state of abjection. Through engagement with Black joy, both in private and online spaces, proponents convey a holistic recognition of Black life, one characterized by moments of exuberance and gratification alongside persistent denigration and violence. Rather than cancelling each other out, these states of being co-exist in ways that accurately summarize what it means for many people to navigate life as a Black person in societies shaped by anti-Black racism.

In practical terms, Black joy can be understood as a resource that enables survival. As Cruz makes clear, its healing capacity when experiencing racism-induced despair and depression can be life-altering and, potentially, lifesaving. Black joy can also facilitate future anti-racist work by sustaining the people who currently drive it and encouraging future generations to act. Marches, picket lines and protests that promote joy by encouraging dancing, singing and chanting affirmative action cries can generate the energy needed to sustain these acts and ensure their future repetition.

Whilst writing this book, I was confronted by moments of sadness, anger and despair that, at times, halted its progression and made me question its direction. With each new chapter came a sobering awareness of the fact that I would have to immerse myself in the details of that chapter's principal case study – one that I knew would viscerally demonstrate the harmful consequences of systemic racism. Seeing visual footage of the victim (often taken posthumously) and subsequent testimonies from their families and friends, reading detailed accounts of the moments and circumstances leading up to their death, and hearing legal rationales and testaments from people who directly blamed the victim for their premature death required a stamina that I was not always able to maintain. For case studies that did not result in death but, instead, brought about a form of 'death-in-life' for that person and their families, immersing myself in testimonies that both justified and commended their pain was both viscerally repugnant and emotionally laborious. The spiritual deflation I often felt while doing this work meant that taking breaks from it became both a necessary part of protecting my own health and a vital means of finishing this book.

While taking these breaks, I often found myself searching for, and scrolling though, online content that demonstrated Black and Brown joy. I watched romantic comedies that featured all-Black casts, YouTube videos that highlighted Black and Brown success, and short clips of Black children laughing and playing with each other seemingly unburdened by racism. When writing the chapter on Alan Kurdi, I searched for images showing migrant compassion and solidarity, and when writing the chapter on Roxane Gay I reminded myself of Gay's sharp humour, poise and social dexterity. This pivot towards joy was instinctive and I did not know that I was using it for medicinal purposes until much later in the writing process. When I returned to each chapter after taking these breaks, I felt restored enough to continue doing the work that I felt was important. By acknowledging these personal challenges, I do not wish to present my responses to this work as unique or suggest that I was unequipped for them. The privileges I was afforded while doing this work were multiple, and in many ways served as a buffer against its full potential impact. Rather, I seek to highlight the importance of recognizing the medicinal purposes of joy when used in service of anti-racist action, and to underscore the need for joy in sustaining it. Without joy, it is difficult to maintain momentum which, in turn, reduces the likelihood of achieving the end goal of racial justice. An important facet of striving towards this end goal lies in our collective ability to sustain ourselves and each other, and this cannot be done in the absence of joy and its accompanying feeling of hope.

All lives (should) matter

The phrase 'all lives matter', often used as a retort by those who oppose the Black Lives Matter movement, has been widely criticized for promoting a post-racial ethos that overlooks how precarity, vulnerability and violence are unevenly distributed along racial lines. When used, this phrase denies, obscures and distorts the harmful effects of racism on the daily lives of those who endure it. While all lives *should* matter certain lives are seen to either *not matter at all* or *matter less* than others. As the case studies in this book have shown, grievability is unevenly determined by media outlets, law enforcement officers, government officials, public institutions, health practitioners and policy makers in ways that make clear the value ascribed to some lives over others. As I hope to have demonstrated throughout this book, grievability is principally concerned with highlighting this differential (dis)regard for human life. The open question of when all lives will matter can be understood as a critique of contemporary grievability politics.

Butler indirectly addresses the role of contemporary biopolitics in bestowing or withholding grievability in their essay 'Bodies that Still Matter'. In this essay, Butler argues that, while it might be preferable to simply state that every life is grievable and to ruthlessly defend that position, doing so overlooks the ways in which certain lives are protected from harm while others are exposed to it, as well as the lethal consequences of that exposure. They write,

> We might prefer to avoid all this complexity and simply say that every life is grievable, and militate for an understanding of that basic equality. That is a good humanist solution and it has merits. But it cannot describe the radical form of inequality that must be challenged. We may want to insist that 'every life is grievable' is a descriptive claim, that all existing life is equally grievable, but if we let that be the full extent of our description, we badly misrepresent present reality. 'Every life is grievable' makes sense politically only if that is a call, a demand, and an explicit aspiration in a world in which structures of radical inequality are rampant.
>
> (Butler 2021: 187)

By saying 'all lives are grievable' or 'all lives matter', proponents gloss over the myriad cracks in systems, structures and institutions that are in desperate need of repair. To make either statement in response to calls for equality is, by implication, to suggest that equality has already been achieved and that no further effort is needed to realize it. In other words, it suggests that the world is already as it should be, which also suggests that further social justice efforts are not needed. Butler makes clear through their reflections that arguing for a recognition of universal grievability can only prove fruitful if it is enacted as a call for equality that has not yet been realized.

Statements affirming that all lives (ostensibly) matter do nothing to advance or support anti-racist efforts that strive for racial justice. When discussing this topic with my students, I often refer to clinical appointments that patients schedule to address a particular medical concern. If a patient were to visit their healthcare provider with a specific complaint of pain in one of their joints and was then told by that healthcare provider that all their joints mattered they would likely respond with frustration. This frustration would not arise from their reaction to a perceived untruth – *of course* all their joints matter – but rather to the inadequate response they have been given to address the specific cause of their pain. The health practitioner's response fails to address the problem at hand, and that is the one in need of remedy. Without a targeted intervention to address their specific joint pain that pain will likely continue.

Other anti-racist advocates have different analogies to explain the fruitlessness and harm embedded in collective statements like 'all lives matter.' A common one involves other health conditions that require (at least initially) a targeted intervention rather than a holistic one. Perhaps the clearest and most effective example is that of cancer activism. If I develop breast cancer and I am principally concerned with reducing the high number of people who are predicted to develop breast cancer in the future I am unlikely to be chastised for any activist work I do which seeks to prevent breast cancer and excludes other types of cancer that are equally important. By focusing on one type of cancer, I am not denying that all types of cancer are harmful and that developing treatments to eradicate all of them matters. Rather, I am prioritizing one that is currently causing crisis and requires immediate intervention.

When it comes to health, unequal investment in the well-being of some over others reveals how grievability is both governed and enacted. Health-promoting resources that are costly, impractical or otherwise inaccessible to those who are most marginalized work to sustain health inequity by directly investing in the lives of some and not in the lives of others. This can be inadvertent and is routinely driven by the assumption that these resources *are* ostensibly available to all. Popular digital applications that offer access to guided meditations, well-being podcasts and calming music aim to promote health in ways that are self-directed, self-determined and self-empowering. By giving users access to these resources as and when they need them, these applications arguably promote a useful stopgap for people with limited access to therapy and/or other forms of mental health care. Additionally, they are often culturally inclusive and offer a range of resources that are tailored to specific groups that are differentially exposed to a range of issues, including racism, sexism and homophobia.

When these interventions are framed as being universally applicable and inclusive, it is important to ascertain the full extent of their accessibility. If they require payment, access to digital technology or digital literacy they are, by default, *exclusive* and, therefore, cannot be seen by themselves to promote health equity. That is not to say that they are not important, useful, and (in some cases) lifesaving resources for many, but rather to suggest that they are not typically designed in ways that are mindful of different forms of precarity. Moreover, they can risk further entrenching health inequity through a biopolitical strategy that promotes the health of some while overlooking the health of others. What is needed is a range of interventions that promote health equity by ensuring universal access to the resources required to live a healthy life. These interventions, in turn, must be mindful of the fact that 'good health' is often subjective and can mean different things to different people. Imagining lives that are universally grievable, then, involves radical imaginings of what these interventions might look like and how they might offer an alternative vision of a future governed by equitable access to diverse health-promoting resources.

It is both unjust and nonsensical to suggest that everyone has access to health-promoting resources that, if used, would decrease their risk of life-threatening disease and increase the likelihood of them achieving 'good health.' For proponents of this claim, various social determinants of health (including racism, sexism, adequate housing and access to green space) are seen as matters of individual responsibility. For some, this means advocating for minimal state investment in expanding access to these resources, and a greater emphasis on strategies that promote self-determination. There is further injustice in suggesting that, when these resources are not used, that lack of use reflects the moral inclinations of the person or group in question rather than the inaccessibility of those resources. To suggest that all people have access to health-promoting resources and some choose not to use them is to suggest that all people who directly develop ill health by not using them do so through their own volition. When it comes to grievability, people who develop ill health and die from avoidable causes risk condemnation from people who view their condition within the framework of deservedness. This framework, in turn, overlooks how inequality governs access in favour of an idealistic assumption that equal access is available to those who work hard enough to achieve it.

It is a simple truth that all lives cannot matter until Black lives also matter. To argue against this truth is to suggest that Black lives are not lives, which reifies the need for movements that seek to counter this argument. It is also a simple truth that Black and Brown people are disproportionately exposed to harms that reduce not only their lives but also their capacity for living. Conceptualizing Black joy and beauty as anti-racist methods offers a self-affirming way to move beyond surviving to thriving. Both also provide avenues through which grievability can be asserted and demanded. However, anti-racist strategies at individual and communal levels should not be mistaken for solutions to the wider problem of systemic racism. What is needed are interracial efforts to insist on a collective recognition of equal grievability that counteracts prevailing ideas that assign worth to economic, social and political value.

Instead of upholding a post-racial ethos that presupposes equal grievability, we must reckon with how and why grievability is differentially distributed along racial lines. Only then can we lay the groundwork for racial health equity and begin implementing our radical imaginings of what could be otherwise. It is my hope that this book will play a part in establishing that foundation by challenging sceptics to consider the material realities that racism produces and pushing the reader to consider why these realities remain entrenched and often go unchallenged. Only when we reach this understanding can we, in Butler's words, 'move from what is to what ought to be, or at least start that movement, which posits a utopic horizon for our work' (Butler 2021: 187).

References

Butler, J. (2021), 'Bodies That Still Matter'. In *Bodies That Still Matter: Resonances of the Work of Judith Butler*, edited by H. Annemie, K. Kwastek and R. Can den Oever, pp. 177–93. Amsterdam University Press.

Cruz, K. (2023), *The Black Joy Project: A Literary and Visual Love Letter to How We Thrive*. Mariner Books.

Hirsch, A. (2018), *Brit(ish): On Race, Identity and Belonging*. Vintage.

hooks, b. (2015), *Sisters of the Yam: Black Women and Self-Recovery*. Routledge.

Hurston, Z. N. (2023), *You Don't Know Us Negroes and Other Essays*. HarperCollins Publishers.

Lorde, A. (1988), *A Burst of Light: Essays*. Firebrand Books.

Morrison, T. (2007), *The Bluest Eye*. Vintage.

Sharpe, C. (2023), *Ordinary Notes*. Daunt Books.

Ward, J. W. and R. J. Butler. (2008), *The Richard Wright Encyclopaedia*. Greenwood Press.

Index